AUTHOR: CAROLYN M

"GUIDELINES FOR WRITING SUCCESSFUL GRANT PROPOSALS FOR NONPROFIT ORGANIZATIONS"

Jumpstart Your Vision!

- ➤ See the Vision!
- ➤ Write the Vision!
- ➤ Think the Vision!
- ➤ Do the Vision!
- ➤ Write a Successful Grant Proposal
- ➤ Finding Funding Resources

A basic guide for beginner grant writers

AuthorHouse™
1663 Liberty Drive
Bloomington, IN 47403
www.authorhouse.com
Phone: 1-800-839-8640

©2010 Carolyn M. Driver, MA. All rights reserved.

No part of this book may be reproduced, stored in a retrieval system, or transmitted by any means without the written permission of the author.

First published by AuthorHouse 10/15/2010

ISBN: 978-1-4520-6556-4 (e)
ISBN: 978-1-4520-6554-0 (sc)

Library of Congress Control Number: 2010911982

Printed in the United States of America

This book is printed on acid-free paper.

Because of the dynamic nature of the Internet, any Web addresses or links contained in this book may have changed since publication and may no longer be valid. The views expressed in this work are solely those of the author and do not necessarily reflect the views of the publisher, and the publisher hereby disclaims any responsibility for them.

"GUIDELINES FOR WRITING SUCCESSFUL GRANT PROPOSALS FOR NONPROFIT ORGANIZATIONS"

Jumpstart Your Vision!

What is your purpose? What is the real problem? What is the cause? What is your mission? What is the solution? How can you make the communities and lives of people you are proposing to serve better? How will the community and people benefit from your proposed funding? How much funding do you need?

See the Vision!

Think the Vision!

Understand the Vision!

Believe the Vision!

Enlarge your Vision!

Connect your Vision with the funder!

Write the Vision!

Do the Vision!

Preface

Guidelines for writing successful grant proposals for nonprofit organizations, is written to provide beginner grant seekers with the knowledge and skills to write a successful grant proposal. It is a beginner's guide to help the grant seeker whose vision, mission, goals and objectives are to provide much needed community services and resources to communities where voids in services have been identified. It is aimed at providing human services to youth, teens, adults, and the elderly populations. It is also geared towards prevention awareness education, social services, health programs and services, training programs, recreation, elimination of poverty programs, employment recruitment and career training, and community development outreach programs. Christian-faith based organizations and other religious groups can also benefit from this book.

Proposal writing is a skill that is learned and acquired through education and experience in the field. It is also an art where creative writing abilities are an asset to a grant writer. It requires brainstorming ideas and thinking out of the box. It is also technical. A glossary of terms has been provided for this reason. There are certain principles and methods that can serve to refine and improve the ability to prepare convincing and persuasive proposals. There are thousands of public and private foundations, corporations, large and small businesses, as well as federal, state, and local government agencies that provide grants in the social services and community services field.

As a grant writer, you will need to answer the following questions. What is your vision, purpose, and mission? What is the real problem? What is the cause? What is the solution? How can you make communities and lives of people you are proposing to serve better? How will the community and people benefit from your proposed funding? How much funding do you need?

This book will teach the new beginning grant writer strategies for writing a successful proposal. There are workbook sheets in several of the chapters that will allow you to fill in the blanks. You will be guided through the process that will hopefully build your confidence in writing a grant proposal.

The book discusses the legal documentation that is needed to be considered a nonprofit organization. Most funders will require proof of your organization having a tax exempt status letter from the IRS. This is discussed in the book. Also discussed is the following: You will learn how to conduct a SWOT Analysis of your nonprofit organization, learn how to write a compelling statement of need for funding, how to establish relationships with funders, program development, the evaluation process for eligibility for receiving funding, finding funding resources, how to write an effective and reasonable budget, how to develop a grant writing team, how to write a letter of intent to apply for funding, suggestions on how to sustain funding, how to measure and evaluate your program for its effectiveness, designing an evaluation survey tool for program participants, how to turn your no into a yes if your proposal is rejected, how to match your interest with the funder, and how to package your proposal before submitting it to the funder.

"Create and leave a legacy that will help and empower others to realize their purpose in life and reach their own personal destiny. Without a vision, you can't plan a future".

Carolyn Driver

About the Author

Carolyn Driver, studied grant writing at the University of Southern California (USC) in 1983. Since her graduation from USC in 1983, she has been writing successful winning grant proposals. She has been a consultant for nonprofit organizations writing grant proposals. Every grant proposal she has written has been funded. She was also an employee in various nonprofit organizations as a grant writer and a quality assurance manager. She has also provided educational grant writing seminars for the private sectors. She specializes in writing grant proposals for public monies which includes federal, state, city, and county grant proposals.

She has helped nonprofit organizations to obtain more than $5 million dollars in grant funding, and has been featured in newspaper articles, as well as on national television and radio stations.

She holds an Associate of Arts degree in early childhood development education, a Bachelor of Science degree in Gerontology, and certification in Public Administration. She also holds a Master of Arts degree in Organizational Management in business. She has twenty years of experience and expertise in the field of management for nonprofit organizations.

She founded a nonprofit organization in the State of California named "Youth Organized and United for Community Action Network" in 1986. She wrote all of her own grant proposals which were all funded by the State of California Department of Education. The funding was used to educate students in grades k-12, their parents, as well as the school district teachers and administrators, about drug and gang prevention.

She has not only written many successful grant proposals for nonprofit organizations, but has also served on several grant writing review teams and made recommendations for funding worthy projects for many nonprofit organizations. She has been on both sides of the grant writing process. She has written successful grant proposals and she has sat on committees to review and award grant proposals for nonprofit organizations in the States of California and Georgia.

She has also written successful grant proposals for Public Housing Authorities in the State of Georgia.

Contents

Preface	vii
About the Author	ix
Author's Acknowledgments	xiii
Who Would Benefit From Buying and Using This Book?	xiv
Who Are The Grant Seekers?	xv
Introduction	xvii
Guide To Using This Book	xxii
Chapter 1. Grant Writing Preparation Process	1
Chapter 2. Goals and Objectives	45
Chapter 3. Letter of Intent to Apply for Funding	49
Chapter 4. Statement of Need	57
Chapter 5. Establishing Relationships with Funder	64
Chapter 6. Method Component	67
Chapter 7. Evaluation Component	74
Chapter 8. Creating Your Title or Cover Page	84
Chapter 9. Program Development	88
Chapter 10. Capability Statement	101
Chapter 11. Budget Component	110
Chapter 12. Budget Audits	122
Chapter 13. Developing a Grant Writing Team	125
Chapter 14. Sustainability Component	131
Chapter 15. Executive Summary	134
Chapter 16. Submitting Your Proposal to the Funder	137
Chapter 17. Funder's Decision	147
Chapter 18. Funding Resources	152
Conclusion	163
Appendix: Glossary/Grant Terminology	166
Bibliography	181

Author's Acknowledgments

To my dear mother Pearl Williams, I thank and credit you for my life of spirituality, faith, love, support, guidance, core values, character, courage, high self-esteem, confidence to believe in myself, education, professionalism, ambition, security, and for giving me hope for a better life. I thank you for all your prayers.

Thanks to my entire family for their prayers, encouragement, love, support, belief, and confidence in me to write this book.

To my daughter Cynthia Marie Driver, I credit and thank her for her computer assistance expertise. I continue to strive hard to be a positive role model for her.

To my son William Driver Jr., thanks for your helpfulness, encouragement, and support.

I thank William Driver, Sr., for his helpfulness, encouragement, and support throughout my colledge education while attending the University of Southern California (USC).

To my daughter-in-law Janolyn Driver, thanks for your time and energy for editing this book.

To Dr. Alvin V. Griffin, M.D., thanks for your encouraging words, support, and belief in me.

To Ebony Walker, thank you for assisting with the editing of this book.

I credit my alumni, the University of Southern California (USC) in Los Angeles, for providing me the education in writing successful winning grant proposals.

Thanks to all of the editors of this book. Thanks to all those people who contributed to the production of this book. I thank AuthorHouse Publishing Company for all of their help and support with this book.

I thank all those who provided help in making my dream become a reality with the writing of this book.

I thank God for the "favor" in my life. I credit God for equipping and empowering me with the vision, strength, ability, confidence, talent, skill, knowledge, and courage to write this book.

I dedicate this book to my grandsons Ryan and Joshua Driver who are the love and joy of my life.

It is my hope that this book will be a blessing to those individuals and nonprofit organizations that wish to make a difference in the lives of people from all walks of life, nationally and internationally around the world.

To God Be the Glory!

Who Would Benefit From Buying and Using This Book?

- Clergy-Faith Based Organizations, Pastors, Bishops, Youth Pastors, Missionaries, Evangelist, and Ministers
- Professionals who work in Non-profit Organizations
- Public school district administrators, School teachers, Principals, Vice-Principals, School Counselors,
- Managers, department heads, and supervisors in non-profit organization
- Private school administrators and teachers
- Christian school administrators
- Business People, Entrepreneurs, Marketing Directors, Salespeople
- Community Leaders
- Social Workers
- Mental health workers, counselors
- Health Care Professionals, physicians, physical therapist, occupational therapist
- Hospital Administrators
- Researchers, Scientists
- Educators
- Pre-school owners, educators
- College Students
- Artist
- Nursing Home Administrators
- Law Enforcement Personnel- Police Departments, Correctional facility administrators:
- Federal, City, State, and County personnel staff
- Any person who has an interest in learning how to write grant proposals

Who Are The Grant Seekers?

GRANT SEEKERS ARE:

- **Non-profit organizations**
- **Public school districts, private schools**
- **Colleges and Universities**
- **Public Agencies**
- **Churches, religious groups**
- **Performing arts, music, drama**
- **Scientists**
- **Artists**
- **Writers**
- **Medical Institutions**
- **Law Enforcement Agencies**
- **Social service agencies**
- **Libraries**

Introduction

Guidelines for writing successful grant proposals for nonprofit organizations, is written to provide beginner grant seekers with the knowledge and skills to write a successful grant proposal. It is a beginner's guide to help the grant seeker whose vision, mission, goals and objectives are to provide much needed community services and resources to communities where voids in services have been identified. It is directed towards proposals that are geared towards providing human services to youth and teens, education, social services, health programs and services, Christian-based organizations, cultural activities, training programs, recreation, elimination of poverty programs, employment recruitment and training, programs and services for the elderly, and community development outreach programs.

Proposal writing is a skill that is learned and acquired through education and experience in the field. It is also an art where creative writing abilities are an asset to a grant writer. It is also technical. A glossary has been provided for this reason. There are certain principles and methods that can serve to refine and improve the ability to prepare convincing and persuasive proposals. There are thousands of foundations as well as federal, state, and local government programs that provide grants in the social services and community services fields.

Large numbers of corporations provide grants for research, training and public service programs through corporate gifts and corporate public and private foundations. There are billions of dollars granted to worthy programs and projects from governmental sources as well as local businesses.

Today with the current availability and wave of computer technology, there are a number of resources available for grant seekers to identify potential funders. Finding potential funders can be frustrating, challenging, and confusing as well as very time consuming. The grant seeker must have patience and be persistent in their search for funding. Your hard work will pay off. With the resources of the internet, and other technology media most grant seekers can research at their own pace and find potential funders whose goals and visions connect with the grant seeker and the funder.

Many people feel that they cannot write a proposal. However, this book will provide guidelines, instructions, explanations, and practice worksheets where the beginner grant writer can fill in the blanks. This will allow the grant writer an opportunity to practice writing their first proposal. Suggestions or recommendations are made that will assist the grant seeker with writing a winning grant. Every grant writer will have their own unique and creative writing style. The proposal writer must have excellent writing skills. The proposal should be written in an effort to persuade the funder that their program and activities mentioned in the proposal have merit. The proposal writer should show the funder the level of promise and commitment to all planned activities. The proposal must be written with clarity and be concise so that the funder will understand how your goals and objectives for your proposed activities or programs are going to be planned, developed, implemented and administered.

Special attention has to be placed on the quality, preparation and the final proposal presentation that will be provided to the funder. Some proposals are simple and very short, for example, foundations or corporate gift applications may only require an abstract or a 2-5 page proposal, while others can be very lengthy, difficult and tedious as well as very time consuming. Government grant proposals are an example of a more difficult proposal. They can require much more details and can be long, tedious, and time consuming to write. However, it can be a very rewarding experience when you write your first grant proposal and you are awarded the funding. As you begin to write more and more grant proposals, the task becomes much easier. You will gain a lot of knowledge and experience with each grant proposal you write. Grant proposals are very competitive. Therefore, it is imperative that grant proposal writers submit a high quality effective proposal that is convincing to the funder.

For any nonprofit organization seeking funding to operate programs or deliver human services to their communities or a target population of people, a written proposal is usually required to be presented and reviewed by a special Board or Committee who makes the final decision on who the funder wants to allocate funds. A professional grant writer cannot guarantee that a proposal will be funded. Even if you hire someone to write a grant proposal for you, the person hired may be able to guarantee that they can write a grant for you but they cannot guarantee that the grant proposal will be funded. The professional grant writer can send the grant proposal to the funder however; the ultimate decision to fund the grant proposal is still in the hands of the review Board who reads all of the grant proposals that are received by the funder. Every proposal is evaluated by a set of criteria. Grant proposals are rated on a point system using a "rubric form". The proposal that receives the highest score is usually the organization or agency that wins the grant award. The organization that is awarded the funding receives a letter of notification from the funder, informing the organization that their proposal has won the grant award for funding their project.

Many elements of the proposal are taken into consideration by the funder. Therefore, it is important to tap into as many resources such as networking strategies, the use of technology, and collaboration with other agencies for support or assistance. Incorporate skills, principles, and methods that will assist you writing the best grant proposal you can submit for funding. Most government agencies will expect or want the organization seeking funds to be able to show how they collaborate with other non-profit organizations or businesses to assist the organization to accomplish their goals and mission.

Proposals have a language of their own. In this book you will learn terminology that is unique to writing a successful proposal. There are key words that funders look for as they read and review proposals that have been submitted for funding. The materials for this book include an extensive glossary of words and definitions that you will be able to incorporate in your proposal.

In this book, the beginner grant writer will learn strategic methods of networking to strengthen a proposal. Do not feel intimidated by the thought of writing a grant proposal. Anyone with basic writing skills and an understanding of the field for which they are writing the proposal can write a successful grant proposal. A grant writer can feel comfortable writing a grant proposal if they are well organized and have all of the materials and information they need at their disposal to write a compelling proposal. The grant writer must demonstrate a passion for the proposed project. It is important for the grant writer to write a grant proposal in the field they have a lot of knowledge about. It is not good to attempt to write a grant proposal for a project where you know nothing about the field.

During my 20 years of experience of writing grant proposals, I have trained participants in grant writing seminars on how to write grants. I have also assisted people with writing grant proposals who had never written one. These people were frightened in the beginning, but as the process became clear to them, they gained confidence and began to feel very comfortable with writing proposals. They are now able to write grants that can be funded. They were taught how to follow a set of guidelines of a "Request for Proposal" (RFP) which enhanced their skills in writing a successful grant proposal.

Grants are an essential source of support for nonprofit organizations especially for starting new programs and services as well as long time standing organizations. A strong proposal must be well written and well organized. An organization can be awarded large amounts of funding as a result of writing a successful grant proposal. But a word of caution! Most new organizations are in need of immediate funding. If this is the case the organization may have to look at alternative means in order to get funds sooner because a grant application approval can take a much longer time when the funds are needed immediately. Some grant cycles can take as long as six to twelve months to receive funding after the proposal has been submitted depending on the funding cycle of the funder. Some funding cycles are shorter. Again, it depends on the funder. Therefore, alternative methods may need to be employed to raise money for the proposed project. Having community fundraisers requesting donations from contributors of local residents and businesses are a good alternative while waiting for funds from a grant proposal award.

Grant proposal writing is only one technique to raise funds for nonprofit organizations. There are several other methods in which to raise funds. The private sector is another source of funding nonprofit organizations. Corporate gifts and also funding from private foundations is another resource for raising funds for non-profit organizations. Governmental agencies such as the federal government, the State, County, and City governments can also provide funding for nonprofit organizations. The proposal writer should always make sure that the funds needed for services and programs are cost effective and reasonable. The need of the funds should be very clear to the funder. Government agencies prefer to fund projects, programs, or services that can be replicated for the least amount of money. Yet the program must be efficient, effective, and a positive benefit to the target population. Government funding can range in the billions of dollars for projects, programs, or social services where there is a proven need for such funding. Grant proposals written must demonstrate how the funds will provide for the betterment of a target population or community.

This book also gives some background information of what is needed to be considered a nonprofit organization. It will discuss the comparisons between a "for-profit" versus a "nonprofit" organization. Both of these business organizations have different characteristics.

This book also discusses the eligibility requirements for nonprofit organizations to receive funding from various funding sources such as foundations, corporations, and governmental agencies in the USA. As stated at the beginning of this book, the focus will be on grant seeking for nonprofit organizations.

This book focuses on requesting funding for nonprofit organizations only. It will not deal with writing grant proposals of funding "for- profit businesses". In order to be eligible to write grant proposals for nonprofit organizations, there are certain steps that need to be in place first. There are legal documents that the nonprofit organization must first obtain from government agencies where the organization is located. The organization must meet all of the legal issues and requirements of the funder and must also be aware of any policy issues that the funder may have.

The organization must have a board of directors who will oversee the business of the nonprofit organization. The organization's executive staff must get approval by the board officials of the organization and be given the authority to write and submit a grant proposal to a funder whether it is a private or public foundation, a corporation, or government agencies.

Grant seekers needs to understand the difference between fundraising and grant seeking. Fundraising is different from seeking a grant in that fundraising does not involve a formal written grant proposal or a grant application process. In fundraising, the organization states what they want. They don't necessarily have to state a real problem. The organization may have a desire for something that is on their wish list or have a particular need or desire but it is not a problem that needs a formal grant proposal for funding. If the organization wants to raise money for a specific project such as a scholarship program for students who are graduating from high school, the organization can simply ask for donations. Letters can be written and mailed out to prospective donors or contributors. Soliciting funds for a fundraiser can also be done by telephone calls and through technology media such as the internet or personal solicitation face-to-face. In fundraising there is more direct contact with the donor as opposed to grant seeking. Some fundraising activities are not focused on funding cycles. Funds are acquired much sooner than with a grant proposal. The preparation and time frame is different in fundraising than in grant seeking. A fundraiser can be planned at any given time throughout the year to raise money for a specific purpose or cause. Fundraisers are not usually on a funding cycle. Grant applications are usually on a funding cycle for government funding. Some well known national organizations have a standard set time of year to hold fundraising events.

In contrast, when an organization is seeking a grant to fund a specific project, the organization must identify a real problem in a target population or community. Grant funds are used to solve problems. Many government agencies will provide funds to find solutions to problems. Private foundations and corporate gifts are used to provide solutions to problems. Grant proposals are more time consuming as this form of requesting funding has some political implications if funding is being requested from a government agency and it also depends on the funding cycle of the funder.

In order to write a successful grant proposal, several essential components are necessary. First you must understand your vision, purpose, and mission. Next, you must know your target population and community. Finally, you must understand how to accomplish your goals and objectives. If you know the problem you want to solve, what you want to do, where you want to do it, and how much the project or program may cost, you have enough information to get started with writing a successful grant proposal.

The terms project or programs can be used depending on the organization and the task that is being undertaken. Be consistent with the term you want to use. Use the term either program or project throughout your proposal.

Good luck. Enjoy the journey. Dreams do come true!

Guide To Using This Book

This book consists of eighteen chapters. It is aimed at providing a guide to the first time beginning grant writer. It is an introduction to the field of proposal grant writing. If you are an inexperienced grant writer and writing your first grant proposal, you may have to read this entire book. However, if you have some experience in grant writing you may be able to skip some sections of this book. Each chapter will provide guidelines and explanations to assist the grant writer in writing a successful grant proposal. Some chapters will have practice worksheets that the grant writer can fill out to help guide the process. Some chapters will have exhibits showing examples of specific documents needed by the funder such as budgets and also legal documents required to be a nonprofit organization.

This book is not written in extensive detail for nonprofit organizations as it would be too much information for a first time grant writer. I didn't want to overwhelm the new beginner grant writer with too much information. The goal of this book is to introduce grant writing to those interested in learning how to write grant proposals, while providing them with a guide in the process.

This book is very basic and hopefully easy to understand. I want this book to be user friendly and not stressful or intimidating for the new beginner grant writer. With practice, the new grant writer will become more confident in their skills as a writer and will become very proficient in writing successful grant proposals.

Chapter 1:
Grant Writing Preparation Process

The difference between nonprofit verses for-profit organizations:

A for-profit organization is a business whose goal is to generate a profit for its owners. There are usually shareholders involved. The tax structure is different. They are not exempt from federal income tax filing. A for-profit business is operated totally different from a nonprofit organization. A nonprofit organization does not have owners or shareholders to distribute profits to. When the nonprofit organization has excess funds, the organization may make contributions to churches or other religious groups, and community programs or projects where there is a void or lack in human services. A nonprofit organization can make distributions to other organizations that qualify as exempt organizations under Section 501 (c) (3) of the Internal Revenue Code of USA. Nonprofit organizations are formed to provide programs, services, and projects to benefit disadvantaged individuals, the poor, and communities in need. They are also formed for other specific purposes.

Writing your nonprofit organization's "Vision Statement"

What is the vision for the organization? Webster defines "vision" as something seen in a dream or having foresight. Webster's New Pocket Dictionary (2000). First decide if it is your personal vision or is it the vision of the nonprofit organization. The vision is not about you personally. The vision should focus on how you are going to meet the needs of the "people" you want to serve. The vision is about the people in need! For the sake of this book, it is important to not confuse your personal vision or dream with the vision of the nonprofit organization. Think about why the nonprofit organization was formed in the first place. Since nonprofits are usually organized or formed to benefit individuals of a target population or community, the funder must have a clear and concise understanding as to the commitment of the proposed project or programs. The vision should state what the organization is committed to do for the target population they want to provide services or programs for. The **"Vision" must be clear.**

It should be a positive statement. Avoid negative statements in your vision statement. Discuss the opportunities of how the organization is going to enhance or add value to the lives of people and communities with the funding in the proposed grant application. Discuss what your organization has done in the past with success. Also discuss what the organization plans to do in the future to further its commitment to improve lives and communities. Think about the problem you want to address in your organizations proposal and how your organizations proposed project is going to fix the problem. Think about solutions that will truly benefit your target population, "the people" and the community.

Writing your "Mission Statement"

State the mission for your organization. Write your mission statement with clarity. State what kind of business the nonprofit organization is. Is it a school for teaching children? Is it a university? Is it a medical or scientific business? Is it a religious organization or church to do ministry? Is it a social service agency? Is it a professional organization? What is the purpose of your organization? Tell the funder in your proposal how the community will be better as a result of the implementation of the organizations programs, services, or projects that are being proposed for funding.

When writing your organizations mission statement, think about the problem your organization wants to address in the proposal. For example, if there is a high crime rate in the communities of the proposed area you want to implement your project, first state the cause of the problem, then discuss how your organization would reduce the crime rate. What action would you take to focus on your target population?

State the problem: Example- There is a high crime rate among teens ages 13-19 in our community. The mission statement should have a solution to the problem. First state the real problem, then state your organizations solution or solutions to the problem. State very clearly how your organization plans to reduce the crime rate. Be very specific in your strategy to resolve this problem being addressed.

Mission statement example: Crimes committed by teens will be reduced or eliminated in our community by providing positive alternatives.

State the problem: Another example- There is an extremely high increase in teen pregnancy in the community of the proposed target area. The cause might be due to the fact that teens are not educated in the area of pregnancy prevention education in school or at their home. The action or solution of the organization could be offering teen prevention education classes at their local high school where the teens attend or teen pregnancy classes could be held at a local community center facilitated by health care professionals or educators in the field of health education. Both teens and their parents can be invited to attend the teen pregnancy health education classes at the neighbor community center.

Mission statement example: To decrease teen pregnancy rate in the community by providing quality health education that will enlighten and empower teens to make wise choices to fulfill their destiny.

Goals: State what major steps your organization will take to accomplish the mission. When a funder looks at goals, they are looking to see what benefits the recipients of your organization target population will gain. Funders prefer to award grants to projects or programs that will have positive substantial benefits to a target population. "A goal is a broad based statement of the ultimate result of the change being undertaken". (Carlson, M. 2002).

In the example given of implementing a teen pregnancy prevention education program, the benefits would be to teens ages 13-18. Due to the teen prevention education program, teens will be more aware of the consequences of teen pregnancy. The goal would be that there would be a big reduction in teen pregnancies as a result of the teen pregnancy prevention education program. Teens would make better life choices. Their education would not be interrupted in high school due to teen pregnancy. Teens would gain knowledge as to the responsibilities that would be placed on them as a young parent at an early age. The ultimate goal is: To reduce the incidence of teen pregnancy by offering teen prevention education classes at the high school level in their community.

Objectives:

"Objectives are the measurable, shorter-term outcomes" (Brown & Brown 2001). The objectives state who, what, when, and how achievement is measured. Discuss who will participate or be involved in the project or activity. This is your target group. Discuss what services or programs are going to be implemented. Discuss the time frame, and explain how you will measure or assess your achievement. The terms: to increase or to decrease shows some measurable level of change to an outcome objective. Discuss what your expected outcome will be at the end of the grant period.

Example: To reduce the teen pregnancy rate in the community by 85% during the first year.

Discuss the problem: Show evidence of the problem. For example, school records, statistics, medical records information, police department crime statistics from local law enforcement agencies, information obtained from social service agencies, surveys, and questionnaires are all materials that can prove a real problem among a target population or in a community.

Needs Assessment:

A needs assessment is a survey. Conduct a needs assessment survey of the targeted population your organization wants to serve. The survey is a list of questions that your target population will answer. After collecting all of the surveys, calculate the results. This is done by using statistics. Listen to the community as they voice their concerns in writing or in a common area where a meeting can be held to get input from the community. The people living in a given community know best what the community needs. Schools have records of data, as well as hospitals, medical facilities, and other social service agencies. Grant writers should not assume what a community needs, but should rely on data collected which clearly will give the grant writer a good idea of a "real problem" that can be addressed in a grant proposal application to seek funding. After the data has been analyzed, now you can focus on the "**REAL PROBLEM**" that has been identified. Address what the causes are of the problem.

What are the "Core Values" of your organization?

What does your organization believe? State your organization's beliefs and philosophies. Clearly state your organizations belief system. Your proposal should express your organizations "values". Your organization must show a strong sense of positive values. This is not where you discuss problems or needs of your organization. Your proposal should stay focused on the organizations core values statements for the funders. It would be difficult for the funder to provide funds to a project where they do not understand what it is you want to do or what the organization is committed to do for the target population or the community you want to serve.

Examples of core values:

- To empower individuals to make sound decisions that will enhance their own personal lives.

- To transform people's lives that will lead to success by providing them with a quality education.

- To help people realize their full purpose and potential in life

- To build cohesive communities that foster unity, productivity, security, safety, good health, and instill a sense of pride.

- To improve the quality of life of people and their community

- To teach and encourage parents to lead by example by exhibiting good character, displaying leadership, demonstrating love, patience, understanding and being a positive role model in the lives of young people.

What is the purpose of your organization?

Define your purpose: Most non-profit organizations are formed for the exclusive purposes for charitable, religious, educational, or scientific purposes. Nonprofit organizations are also formed to meet the needs of less fortunate individuals. Many nonprofit organizations provide relief to the poor, the distressed, and the underprivileged.

State in your proposal what your expectations are in terms of achievements and benefits of your proposed program or project. Explain how the achievements will be accomplished. Explain what the benefits are to the target population whether it is individuals, families, or a community as a result of the funding being sought. The funder is looking to see a high quality proposal that will tell them what you intend to accomplish as a result of them funding your program or project. An example of a purpose could be: In order to reduce the teen pregnancy rate, teen pregnancy prevention and education classes will be offered at the local high school.

What is the Cause of the real Problem? Explain why a funder should fund your organization. Funders or donors prefer to give money to a "specific cause" they are passionate about. For example, if the "cause" is to eliminate hunger in the USA, show how your organization is going to address the problem of hunger in your proposal. Tell the funder what your organization has already done in the past to address the issue of feeding hungry people. Identify the causes of hunger. What is the target population? Why are people hungry?

What is the organizations solution to the problem you are addressing in your proposal?

Describe to the funder the solution or solutions your organization plans to address the problem of hunger. The solution must be realistic and achievable. Be clear in your strategies.

Definition of a proposal:

Definition: "A proposal is a written document that discusses a plan". A plan of proposed activities, services, projects, or programs are presented to a prospective funder. A proposal involves more than one party. It involves the organization seeking funding and the funder. Once the grant writer has completed writing the grant proposal, it is hand delivered or mailed to the funder. Once the funder receives the grant proposal, the funder takes the necessary steps to follow their procedures to inform the grant writer if the grant proposal will be funded. The proposal should be persuasive and convincing to the funder. It should be positive and never negative. The proposal should state the level of commitment to the proposed project or program. The proposal must be written with clarity and very high quality. The proposal should clearly discuss the organization's vision, mission, purpose, goals, and objectives. Discuss how the mission is going to be accomplished. The proposal should match the intense interest of the funder and the organization presenting the grant proposal.

"A proposal serves five functions. It is a written representation of a program, it is a request, it is an instrument of persuasion, it is a promise and a commitment, and it is a plan". (Lefferts, R. 1982).

A grant application Versus A grant proposal: The term "application" is used when the funding source hands you an application either on paper or in electronic format. Cover forms, budget forms, and other information-gathering forms may be included for you to fill in and return with the grant application narrative by a specific due date. A governmental unit, federal, state, or local governments generally issue a grant application and guidelines for completing required sections. (Browning, B. 2001).

A nonprofit organization can write a grant application if the organization has received their 501 (c)(3) tax-exempt determination letter from the Internal Revenue Service (IRS). A nonprofit organization can write a request for funding from government agencies, foundations, and corporations once the organization is deemed to be eligible for grant monies from these organizations. Most foundations, corporations, and governmental agencies require recipients requesting funding to have a 501(c)(3) tax exemption determination letter from the IRS in order to receive funding.

A proposal is usually a more free-flowing grant request. You are free to put your own ideas on paper about your organization and the program or project that you want to fund. (Browning, B. 2001). If you are filling out an application for a foundation for funding, or if your are responding to a "Request for Proposal" for a government agency, the planning and development of the program or project you are seeking funding for is usually the same. The requirements might be a little different depending on the guidelines of the proposal or the application process, but both processes require the same elements to write a successful grant proposal. The application or the request for proposal (RFP) must be written with clarity and be concise of what the organization is seeking funding for. Both must be consistent with good planning, good program development, adequate staffing needs, allocation of resources, and a good implementation plan. You must show a level of commitment, a good dissemination plan, and demonstration of how the program and activities are going to administered and managed.

Elements of a proposal include the following:

(A) A program involves planning, program development, and implementation. Resources need to be identified to carry out the goals and objectives of the program components. Social service, community services, or human service programs are involved in this process.

(B) The organization must request allocation for resources. The organization has to identify funding sources. The proposal should state very clearly why the funds are needed or being requested. The organization interest should match the interest of the funder.

(C) The organization must be political in persuading a funder to support the programs or project the organization is seeking funding for. The proposal must be very convincing that the funds will truly benefit the target population or the community.

(D) The applicant must promise the funder that they will use the funds as stated in the grant proposal. The programs and services must be carried out in a specified period of time. The organization must pay close attention to the cost. Do not exceed spending that the funder has awarded in the grant. Stay within the proposed cost. If the funding is from a government agency, the organization must sign a contract that states what is expected of the organization in terms of contract compliance. The organization signs a contract with government agencies and is expected to adhere to the terms of the contract between the organization and the funding agencies. Once the funding contract has been signed by the organization receiving the grant award, the contract becomes a legally binding agreement between the organization and the funding agency.

(E) The plan will discuss program development in planning of activities, staffing pattern needs, how the program activities are going to be carried out and by whom. The plan discusses management operations of how the program or services are going to be operated from the starting date to the completion date of each activity discussed in the grant proposal. The plan in the proposal specifies all of the activities. The equipment and the facilities are included in the plan. Discuss the kind of equipment that is needed and how much equipment is needed. Explain how the equipment will be utilized during the project or programs. In the planning process, discuss the facility. Where is it located? What type of facility is it? What size is the facility? Will the facility be appropriate to operate the project or programs in? Describe the kind of accommodations exist in the facility to show the capability of handling the programs or services you want to provide. The entire cost that will have a direct impact on the programs and services are discussed. How much the program or services will cost to develop and implement should be discussed. Involved in discussing the cost is how much each item in the budget is going to cost. The plan should have a line item budget presented to the funder. The proposal must show the funder that the organization has a well developed plan for the development, implementation, and administering of all of the activities proposed.

Different types of Proposals:

"There are research proposals, planning proposals, training proposals, technical-assistance proposals, and program proposals". (Lefferts, R. 1982)".

This book focuses on human services program proposals. These proposals deal with services and programs for individuals, families, groups, or communities. However, the other proposal types could overlap into these program proposals. Many family and service oriented proposals provide a component of training, education, planning, and technical assistance. Most proposals still contain the same steps in writing a grant proposal as a program proposal. The guidelines in all proposals are very similar. Some may be different according to specific criteria and context that is needed to carry out the goals, objectives, and mission of the organization stated in the grant proposal.

Solicited and unsolicited grants:

If a nonprofit organization wishes to receive solicited proposal RFP's, the grant writer can contact government agencies and request to have their organization's name put on the government's agencies RFP or bidding mailing list. When funding announcements are made, a notice of funds availability (NOFA) is mailed to each organization on the RFP mailing list. A for-profit and nonprofit organization can solicit a formal request to receive a RFP from the federal government, city, county, state or any local agency. If a non-profit organization receives a solicited RFP for funding and completes the application grant process and is awarded funding, the organization thus enters into a contractual agreement with the funding agency. The organization signs certifications for government oversight for dealing with administrative and employment practices. This is a requirement for all non-profit organizations that are funded by the federal government and other government agencies. Appropriate staff or organization officials can sign certifications for grant proposals. The Executive Director and a department head of the organization can sign certifications. Also anyone selected by appropriate personnel may also sign a certification document.

Some individuals or organizations apply for unsolicited grants. If the individual or organization is funded it is usually a grant that does not have as many constraints as a government grant award. Some unsolicited grants only require 2-5 pages of a narrative proposal with a budget for their proposed activity such as foundations or private individuals or corporate sponsorship. When you write a narrative be sure to add information that will give the funder an idea as to why funds are needed and how the funds will be expended.

Narrative Summary:

Browning, B. (2001) explains that a narrative should include an introduction to the background of the organization when it was founded, its purpose, its mission and its location. Discuss major accomplishments that are relevant to your proposal. If your organization is up and running, discuss your current programs and activities. Discuss the success of your programs. If the program is not in operation yet, discuss your proposed plan of activities. Browning, B. also suggest discussing the demographics of your constituency. Talk about the population to whom your organization will provide services. Include age range, gender, ethnicity, economic status, educational level and other characteristic descriptors. Provide a description of the targeted community you want to provide services to. Include a statement about the problem you want to address. Discuss a compelling statement for the need for funding. Discuss how your organization plans to solve the problem identified. Discuss how you will use the monies if your organization is funded. Also discuss the goals and objectives for your proposed program or project. Discuss a brief evaluation plan.

Remember the narrative is an outline of your entire proposal. It gives the funder a quick overview of what your plan to do for a target population or community. The narrative should be very simple, yet concise to the reader. It should be written with clarity to the funder.

When a grant proposal is submitted to a foundation by a non-profit organization, and funding is awarded by the foundation, the organization receives an award letter and a letter of agreement rather than a formal contract. The same thing holds true for corporate gifts of funding donations.

The process funders use to evaluate grant proposals:

Most funding sources including all federal agencies apply formal criteria in evaluating proposals. All proposals are assigned points for each section of their proposal using a rubric form. The judging is done by a review panel. There is an initial screening first to make sure the applicant meets the criteria to apply for funding. For example, if the funder is announcing funding for a teen pregnancy prevention program and the organization has sent in a proposal for a nutritional program, the proposal for the nutritional program would not be eligible for this round of funding because it is not aligned with the interest of the funding agency. The nutritional proposal would not even be considered by the evaluation team because it did not meet the requirements for the first screening. The majority of proposals are evaluated by a team of people who are familiar with evaluating grant proposal applications.

If a proposal is written to a funder for a teen pregnancy prevention program, the applicant must demonstrate an understanding of the specifics of the teen pregnancy problem and of the delivery of services or conduct research in this field. In the example above, the funder was announcing funding for a teen pregnancy prevention program, the organizations that submit proposals for this announcement will be strongly considered for funding provided the organizations have met all of the requirements stated in the RFP announcement.

The proposal must be written and organized so that the funder can understand the goals, objectives, and mission of the proposed project, service, or activities. The proposal should be an easy document to read. Don't' use slang language or street jargon. The funder may not understand language that is not professional or is ambiguous. Always use language that is understood clearly by anyone reading your grant proposal. Don't use etc. or so forth. Let the funder know that you understand all of the material presented in the proposal.

If a proposal is written in response to an RFP, follow all of the guidelines. Answer all of the questions honestly and truthfully. The proposal should discuss all aspects of the proposed project such as the purpose, objectives of the project, need of the funding, activities, discuss the staffing needs for the project, discuss the management of the project, length of time for the project, and finally discuss the cost of the project. The grant writer should be sure that the proposal covers every item that is specified. Make sure all certifications, addendums, insurance policies, assurances, support letters, Memorandum of Understanding (MOU), Memorandum of Agreements (MOA), are completed, properly executed, and signed by appropriate organization staff or other authorized individuals that have the authority to sign legal documents

Proposals must be responsive to the requirements of the funding agency and must also be responsive to a documented real problem and need. Proposal to government funding agencies must be responsive to all specifications regarding both format and content set forth in the RFP. Example, if the RFP requires a proposal to be submitted on a CD/DVD along with the written proposal, a CD/DVD must be provided with the submission of the proposal. If the RFP specifies that the proposal be written on 8 1/2 x 11 white paper with borders ½ inch on each side of the paper, then this is what is expected. The proposal should also demonstrate that it is responding to a real and documented need in the community, among the group to be served, and or in the general field. The proposal will be strengthened by showing the proposed program is responsive to the interest of those who will be involved. Letters of endorsement and results of surveys and community meetings will serve to document responsiveness to need.

Support letters can be provided by other social services agencies, health establishments for example hospitals, clinics, school districts, religious organizations, civic organizations, and politicians, Survey results can be gathered from a needs assessment of the community. Develop a brief questionnaire to feel the pulse of the community you wish to serve.

Foundations have written guidelines that proposals must meet. Information to enhance responsiveness to the interests of a particular foundation can be provided by examination of foundation reports and other materials. There should be an interest in the same area to address a problem. For example, if the foundation provides educational scholarships to disadvantaged high school students to attend college, the grant seeker needs to submit a proposal to the foundation also seeking funding for scholarship funding for disadvantaged high school students.

Corporations (corporate funders) have special interest. Corporate grants are made to reflect favorably on the corporation. Proposals to corporations should show a connection between the proposed project and the interest of the corporation. Corporations like to fund projects or programs that are community oriented or community based.

The needs statement should be relative to proposed program activities. The goals and objectives should be consistent with all of the proposed activities. The staffing pattern should be of appropriate size. Staff should hold appropriate credentials, training, education, experience, or expertise to fulfill staffing requirements that will provide the highest possible quality of delivery of services. There should be enough staff in terms of numbers of individuals working on the project.

The proposal must have an effective plan to carry out the proposed activities. The proposal is strengthened by indicating that you understand the barriers, problems, and difficulties that must be overcome in order to effectively provide the proposed services and achieve the objectives.

The proposal must convince the funder that the organization can successfully carry out the activities it promises to implement. You can discuss the qualifications of staff to work on the project. Discuss how the agency has handled problems in the past in the proposal. Discuss the experience and history of the organization. Show a track record of past activities and their success rate. Discuss alternative means of funding that will compliment the funding your organization is seeking to perform the programs and services on the proposal. Get testimonials, any thank you notes of acknowledgment, and praise letters expressing the good work that have helped people or communities in the past to strengthen your proposal.

The funder must be reassured that the program or project proposed will be managed in an efficient and effective manner. The organization must have an administrative management team to oversee all of the day to day operations of the proposed project or programs. The grant writer needs to indicate the kinds of managerial and financial systems and controls that will be employed to ensure that the funding is going to be used as stated in the grant proposal. Government agencies require stringent reporting of program activities. Some agencies or funders require monthly reporting while others may require quarterly or annual reports. The Board of Directors of the organization can be provided with monthly reports of how the project is being managed.

Reports must be submitted to the funder in a timely manner by the due date. Penalties may be imposed if reports are submitted late to government agencies. Most funding agencies require reporting requirements for accountability for managerial controls as well as financial accounting. The forming of committees to monitor the activities of the community can be provided with reports about the efficiency of the proposed funding. The grant writer needs to reassure the funder that the organization will follow all of the guidelines for reporting all activities of the proposed project. The reports must be accurate and honest.

A proposal should not overstate its ability to provide programs or services it cannot realistically deliver. The goals and objectives must be realistic for the people you want to serve and the community. Keep the numbers of people you want to serve realistic for the amount of funding that is being sought. Do not ask for more money than is available from the funder. If the grant writer does some research on the funder, the funder can tell the grant writer how much money the funder gives to a non-profit organization for a specific program or project. Some foundations or corporate sponsors will list their annual giving on their annual financial or quarterly reports. Today because of the technology of computers, many corporations will put their annual financial reports on the internet for the public to review.

Grant Preparation Process:

The following is a guide to gathering information for the grant writing process for those who have not formed a nonprofit organization yet. If your organization is already formed you can skip this section of the book. For the purpose of this book, I am referencing the rules and regulations for the State of Georgia in the United States of America (USA). I will also reference information concerning the 501(c) (3) application process for nonprofit organizations in the USA.

Before your organization can apply for funding for your non-profit organization, there are several legal documents that need to be in place first for those individuals who want to write grant proposals for nonprofit organizations. The business operation has to be in place as a nonprofit organization.

Legal documents should be maintained in a safe place in the office of the nonprofit organization.

Sometimes funders will request a copy of some of your organizations documents such as a "tax exempt "determination letter" granted by the IRS before they will fund your organization. All funders do not request a 501(c) (3) tax exempt determination letter but the majority of corporations, foundations, and governmental agencies requires a nonprofit organization to have a tax exempt status letter in order to be eligible to receive funding. Check with the funder for this requirement. The funder will let you know if a tax exempt determination letter is required in order to apply for funding or to submit an RFP application for funding. The grant writer can always call a prospective funder to inquire about what the stipulations or requirements are to request an application or an RFP to request funding for the organization.

Below is a sample of a 501(c) (3) Internal Revenue Service (IRS) nonprofit tax exempt determination letter provided to nonprofit organizations.

Legal documents that are required to be a nonprofit organization

- Obtain an **Employer Identification Number (EIN) form SS-4 from the Internal Revenue Service (IRS) USA**. This is required for both profit and non-profit business organizations in the USA. This is a federal tax identification number. www.irs.gov

- The nonprofit organization should have organizational documents such as the **"Articles of Incorporation"** if the organization has been incorporated. The documents, once approved by the Secretary of State, will be sent to the organization with an official State of Georgia Seal indicating that the documents have been filed by the State. The document will give the date the Article of Incorporation was "filed" by the Secretary of State. The State will issue a certificate of Incorporation with a corporate seal. This process is done in the State of Georgia. Check with the state department where the organization is located concerning corporation requirements.

- Articles of Incorporation states who the Incorporators for the business or organization are. It states the official legal name of the business or organization. It gives the address and the name of the registered agent. The County where the business is located is stated. Check with your State Department where your organization is located if you want to incorporate your business or organization. Different States have different guideline, rules, laws, and regulations requirements.

Recognition of Tax-Exempt Status for Nonprofit Organizations:

Obtain publication 4220 booklet from the Internal Revenue Service. " Applying for 501(c)(3) tax-exempt status". Obtain Form1023 application. Complete the application and mail it back to the IRS with the appropriate fee. This is a federal document in the USA. The application contains instructions on how to complete your application. A checklist is included with the application instructions to assist with the process. Publication 557 discusses the rules and procedures for organizations seeking recognition for exemption from federal income tax under section 501(a) of the Internal Revenue Code. Website: www.irs.gov (2009)

- Apply for a 501(c)(3) tax exempt "determination letter" from the Internal Revenue Service (IRS) in the USA. If the nonprofit organization applied for tax-exempt status by filling out a 1023 form for exemption, the IRS will review the information. If the IRS determines that sufficient information has been provided to the IRS and meets all of the exemption requirements of the IRS, then the IRS will approve the 1023 form application and send the organization a **"determination letter"** notifying the organization of the tax exempt status that has been granted to the nonprofit organization. Contributors will be assured that their donations are tax-deductible. Check with the IRS in the USA if you have questions regarding tax-exempt organizations.

- "Churches that meet the requirements of Internal revenue code (IRC) section 501 (c)(3) are automatically considered tax exempt and are not required to apply for and obtain recognition of tax-exempt status from the IRS. Although there is no requirement to do so, many churches seek recognition for tax-exempt status from the IRS because such recognition assures church leaders, members, and contributors that the church is recognized as exempt and qualifies for related tax benefits. For example, contributors to a church that has been recognized as tax exempt would know that their contributions generally are tax-deductible." (IRS publication 18289 (2009).USA

- It is a wise decision for a church to apply for a 501(c)(3) 1023 IRS "Determination Letter" to be tax-exempt. They are usually considered tax exempt by the mere fact that they are considered to be a church or a religious group. However, there is an advantage for churches to apply for a 501(c)(3) 1023 tax exempt status "Determination Letter" from the IRS because many funders will not fund grant applications without a IRS tax exempt "Determination Letter".

- Foundations, corporations, businesses, other nonprofit organizations, federal, state, city, and county government agencies will require a nonprofit organization to have a tax exempt status to be eligible to apply for and receive funding. This includes churches or other religious organizations. Even an individual donor or contributor may want to see a tax exempt determination letter issued by the IRS in order to make a donation to a church or any other nonprofit organization. Again, it is not mandatory for churches to apply for the 501 (c)(3) tax exempt status determination letter. If a church or other nonprofit organizations expect to write and submit grant applications or proposals for funding, it is strongly recommended that they obtain a "tax exempt determination letter from the IRS. You do not want your funding opportunities to be limited because your church does not have a tax exempt determination letter if it is required by certain funders. Not all funders require a tax exempt determination letter but most funders do request them.

  Donors or contributors are able to write off their donations or contributions on their taxes when they have proof of a tax determination letter from the IRS. Charities that make donations to nonprofit organizations or churches may also require a nonprofit organization to have a tax exempt determination letter issued by the IRS. I had the experience of writing a solicitation letter to a major food corporation seeking food donations for a church to feed community residents for a major holiday. This letter was written on behalf of a church. I explained to the food chain corporation office why I needed funding or food for this special holiday event. The first question I was asked by the corporate office was "does your church have a 501(c)(3) tax-exempt determination letter issued by the IRS? I replied yes. I was informed by the corporation that.it requires all nonprofits to have a "determination letter before they make any donations or contributions to nonprofit organizations. I was asked by the corporation to submit proof of the determination letter from the church. Once I fulfilled the tax-exempt requirement of the corporation, the corporation did make a contribution for the feed the hungry food campaign for the church. The church would not have been able to get the donation from this corporation if the church did not have a tax exempt determination letter from the IRS.

- Section 501(c)(3) organizations are required to keep books and records detailing all activities both financial and nonfinancial. (IRS).

- Obtain IRS Publication number 1771 on "Charitable Contributions for disclosure requirements. This publication explains the federal tax law for organizations such as charities and churches that receive tax-deductible contributions and for taxpayers who make contributions (IRS publication 2009).

- Obtain Publication Charities 4221-PC and 4221-PF, Publication 557, and the instructions to Forms 990, 990-EZ, and 990-PF for information on "record keeping". (IRS publications).

- Obtain Publication 4221 for information about annual information return requirements. From the (IRS).

The above IRS information is not a comprehensive listing of all of the IRS publications for the IRS. You may call the IRS Customer service toll-free at (800) 829-1040 for all questions or information you may have concerning rules, regulations, requirements, tax information, or responsibilities relating to tax exempt organizations. You may also visit the IRS exempt organizations website at www.irs.gov.

Always consult the IRS for any new update information on any publications. Information does change.

Sample internal revenue tax exempt determination letter-USA. This is not a real document. Exhibit is shown for illustration purposes only. The dates and some of the information stated on this letter are fictitious.

	Department of the Treasury
	Employer ID Number:
	01-0000000
	Case Number: XXXXXXXXXX
INTERNAL REVENUE SERVICE	Contact person name:
P.O. BOX 00000	C. X Jones
ADDRESS, NV 00000	Contact phone number:
	(519) 000.0000
Date: January 2, 2012	
Blue-sky Child Development Center	Acct. period ending:
P.O box xxx	12-31-2012
Blue-sky, NV 00000	Charity status:
	555 (0) ()() ()
	Form000 Required
	Yes or No
	Effective date of exemption:
	July 30- 2012
	Contribution deductibility
	Yes
	Addendum Applies
	No

Dear Applicant,

Upon review of your application for tax exempt status, it has been determined that your organization meets the requirements to be considered tax exempt from Federal income tax under section 501 (C)(3) of the Internal Revenue Code. Contributors may deduct contributions to you under section 170 of the Code. You are also qualified to receive tax deductible bequests. You may qualify to be a public charity or foundation. Your charity status is stated above.

Because this letter could help resolve any questions regarding your tax exempt status, you should keep it in your permanent records.
Enclosures:

Sincerely,

Director, IRS sample examiner

To be tax-exempt as described by the IRS under Section 501(c)(3), an organization must be organized and operated exclusively for one or more purposes such as religious, scientific, educational, or other charitable purposes. "None of the net earnings of the organization may benefit any private shareholder or individual. Churches and other religious organizations qualify for exemption from federal income tax and are generally eligible to receive tax-deductible contributions. No substantial part of its activity may be attempting to influence legislation. The organization may not intervene in political campaigns. The organization's purposes and activities may not be illegal or violate public policy. Activities may not be illegal or violate public policy." Check with the Internal Revenue Service (IRS) in the USA for any questions you may have concerning 501 (c)(3) applications or tax exempt status for nonprofit organizations. (Refer to the IRS web site www.irs.gov)

- Register your nonprofit organization with the Secretary of State's Office as a "Charity Organization" if you want to be considered as a charitable organization". You will need to fill out some documents and then the documents will be reviewed by the appropriate office to determine if you meet the criteria to be considered a "Charity". Pay the appropriate fees if there is a fee for this registration. Each State Department has their own policies and procedures for registering as a charity. Check with your State department in your State to inquire about registering as a charitable organization. Each State has different rules, regulations, laws, and guidelines to conduct business. Check with all of your government agencies in the State your organization is located where you operate or intend to operate to find out what you need to do to conduct business as a nonprofit organization. The information provided here is for the State of Georgia therefore, I am giving guidelines for Georgia.

- Written **By-laws** compiled by your board of directors of the non-profit organization. The organizations by-laws govern the operations and management of the nonprofit organization. Make sure your by-laws have been read, discussed, and voted on and adopted by the board of directors and the appropriate chairperson or other designated person such as the secretary has signed the by-laws. The by-laws dictate the operation and management of the running of your organization. Be sure to include a "conflict of Interest policy" in your organizations by-laws. This is a requirement of the IRS.

- Every nonprofit organization must have a board of director or a board of trustees. Be sure your board members or board trustees are in place once the organization is formed. The board members or board trustees are responsible for overseeing the operations of the nonprofit organization. They have voting rights and makes decisions, policies, procedures, and recommendations to the organization. They are the governing body of the organization. They have certain powers and authority as board members or trustees for the organization.

- Complete form C100 for the Securities and Business Regulation Licensing Department Georgia Charitable Solicitations Act Charitable Organization Registration. You can obtain this form from the State Georgia Secretary of State

Office if the nonprofit organization is located in the State of. Georgia. Pay the appropriate fee. Check with the State department your nonprofit organization is located in to find out what their requirements are if any to register as a charity. Every state department has different rules, regulations, guidelines, policies, procedures, requirements, and fees.

- Maintain all of your **certifications or registrations** in a safe place for your nonprofit organization.

- If you are a nonprofit corporation and your organization is incorporated obtain a "Corporate Seal" for your organization. The seal can be purchased at a store that sells office supplies.

- Most non-profit organizations are already formed by the time they want to write grant proposals for funding. The information here is intended for individuals who would like to write grants for funding but have not gone through all of the mandatory required steps to be considered a nonprofit organization. The above information is very basic. It is in no way a complete outline for the entire process of rules, regulations, policies, laws, requirements, procedures, or practices for a non-profit organization. Check with your local government agencies such as City, County, State departments, and the USA Federal government (IRS) for all rules and regulations concerning non-profit organizations. Become aware of compliance requirements. Do not take short cuts in following all of the rules, laws, and policies, requirements for reporting and submitting filings, and regulations that are required to be a nonprofit organization. If you have any questions concerning putting your organization together or how to be in compliance, contact your local and federal governments for any questions you may have. Agency personnel are available to assist you with any concerns or questions you may have throughout the entire process of putting your organization together if you are not a nonprofit organization.

All nonprofit organizations are required to carry liability insurance to protect the corporation, individuals, and the facilities.

After you have formed your nonprofit organization, and all of your legal documentation is in place, you are now ready to start writing grant proposals. Recommendations or suggestions will be provided to you as you begin your journey in writing your grant proposal.

GETTING STARTED TO WRITE A GRANT PROPOSAL:

Obtain a Request for Proposal (RFP) or a grant application from funding sources. Contact the funder and ask to have your nonprofit organization's name placed on the bidder's mailing list to receive request for proposals (RFP's) that you or your organization would be interested to apply for funding.

Bidder's Conference:

A bidder's conference is announced when the RFP is mailed out to prospective grant seekers. If the funder is going to hold a bidder's conference, get the address and the time of the bidder's conference. Sometimes the funder will have the prospective grant seeker to sign up in advance for the conference. Ask the funder if you need to sign up to attend the bidder's conference? A bidder's conference meeting is held shortly after the Request for Proposals has been sent out to interested organizations. At the bidder's conference meeting the grant seeker can ask all the questions they have concerning the RFP process. There are many other nonprofit organizations in attendance at these bidder's conferences. All of the organizations attending the bidder's conference are planning on submitting grant proposals for the same funding your organization is applying for. The competition is very intense. The bidder's conference allows prospective grant writing applicants to meet the funders and ask any questions they may have. Be sure to attend the bidder's conference if one is being offered. It will work to your advantage. It is very informative for prospective grant proposal writers. Be on time. If you are late you will miss information that you may need to write your grant proposal. There is a time period you can call the funder to ask questions after the bidder's conference. Sometimes there is a week after the bidder's conference when you can call the funder and ask questions regarding the RFP application process. This is to benefit grant writers who could not attend the bidder's conference for various reasons. After that time has expired no more questions are answered to be fair to all applicants seeking funding.

Below is a sample of a question that may be asked by a prospective grant seeker at a "Bidder's Conference". Other items of interest are discussed and addressed by the funder at this conference. Suggestions are also provided by the funder at this conference as a guide to assist prospective grant seekers with the grant writing process.

Example of a question by a grant seeker: Does the funder want a letter of intent to apply for this round of funding?

Answer by the funder: Yes. This letter informs the funder that your organization intends to apply for the funding announced in the RFP. This is a time sensitive letter.

If your organization intends to apply for the funding, be sure to write the letter and submit it by the due date. The letter of intent should be 1-2 pages. No more than 2 pages long. No smaller than 11 font size should be used. Follow the instructions provided by the funder.

Use only white paper 8.5 X 11 paper. Avoid using color paper.

- Submit letter of intent to the funder no later than the due date. No exceptions. Write the letter on letterhead stationary representing the organization.

- Letter of transmittal can be the same as letter of intent. Both documents serve the same purpose.

Gathering information:

Gather the following information below in preparation of your grant proposal. Write answers to questions that are being asked for writing your proposal. Write statements that need an explanation. Conduct survey for your needs assessment. Complete task where needed. Follow all of the instructions of the funder requirements. Don't take short cuts in the preparation process. Go through this list and check off each area once you have completed the task.

- What is the organization's "Mission Statement"? Write the statement.

- What is the organization's philosophy? Write the organizations philosophy

- Conduct a needs assessment-Have you conducted your community needs assessment?

- Write a compelling "Need" statement.

- Make sure your grant request matches the goals and objectives of the funder. Both the organization and funder should share the same interest or be compatible in their mission. Research funders on the internet or at a foundation center library.

- Does the funder require an executive summary? If yes, write an executive summary

- The executive summary or sometimes called the cover letter is written when the majority of the proposal is finished. It is best to write the summary at the end because the summary discusses the bulk of the grant.

- Why was the organization formed? Write the answer

- What is the purpose of the organization? Write the answer

- What is the purpose for the funding? How will the funding be used? Write a statement

- How much funding is available? Create a budget

- Who is eligible to apply for the funding? Make sure your organization has the 501(c)(3) nonprofit status to be eligible to request funding

- Authorizing signature is needed to apply for funding. This is done by a CEO or board chairperson of the nonprofit organization. The signature authorizes the grant writer to seek funding.

- What is the number of grants to be awarded? Ask the funder.

- What is the size of the grant being offered by the funder? Ask the funder for the amount.

- Know the funding cycle of the funder. Call the funder and put their funding cycle dates on a wall calendar.

- Call funding agencies to put your organizations name on a mailing list to receive RFP's or grant applications

- What is the format for writing the proposal? Ask the funder.

- If the funder wants the proposal on a disc, be sure to provide the number of disc requested.

- Describe your organization. Write this information

- Give the history and location of the organization. Write this information

- Identify and collaborate with key people, employees, civic leaders, outside organizations

- Give a brief overview of the population you want to serve, age, ethnicity, culture, grade levels, and income level.

- What are the goals and objectives of your program or project? Write this information

- Goals are the long term outcomes of the project, example, to increase literacy education to older adults. Write your goals

- Objectives are the measurable, short-term outcomes, example: objectives can include numbers, such as specified target dates or surveys. Example, to decrease crime among youth in low income areas in 12 months. Write your objectives

- What are your methods to address the problem in your proposal? The method is the means to an end. How will your organization accomplish its goals and objectives? Example, by providing mentoring programs and counseling to at risk youth in low-income communities. Write your response.

- Describe how you are going to accomplish your goals and objectives. Write this information

- Identify the void in your community. Address the "Real" problem. Refer to your needs assessment. Write a statement about the problem you want to address.

- What is the cause of the problem? Write a statement why you think the problems exist.

- Evaluation- How will you measure the success of your program or project? What method(s) will be used? Write your method of how you will evaluate your program or project.

- Proposal submission- When is the proposal due to the funder? Find out what the deadline date is to submit your proposal. Mark your calendar as soon as you receive the RFP. The deadline date will be stated on the RFP along with the time of day it is due. Most proposals are due by the end of the business day for governmental proposals. However, some proposals are due by 12 Noon. It is up to the funding agency as to when a proposal is due. Do not submit the proposal late. Funding agencies will not accept any late proposals regardless of the excuse for why it is late. Proposals are very competitive. If your proposal is submitted late to the funder, your organization is already out of the competition for funding. There are no exceptions. Your proposal will not be considered if it is not postmarked by the due date. Send proposals by certified mail or registered mail as this is the only proof you will have that your proposal was mailed in time.

- Preparation of the cover letter for the grant proposal. Write your cover letter

- Time and commitment- Make sure you have the time and commitment to write a high quality grant proposal. Keep all applications for funding neat and clean. Make copies of the RFP or application when you first receive it from the funder. In the event your RFP or application becomes soiled or ruined you will have a fresh one to apply.

- Ask the funder what will be the "Review Process?

- Responsibilities: Who is going to do what? Who will develop the timeline to get the proposal written?

- Who is the contact person for your organization? This person's name is usually listed on the cover sheet. It may be a department head, director, or officer of the organization. List name.

- Who is the contact person for the funder? Get the name and telephone number of this person.

- Justification- Justify the need for funding. Use statistical data.

- Determine what type of entity you want to get your funding from? For example, foundations, corporations, governmental agencies such as Federal, State, City, or County. Call these agencies and have your organizations name placed on the mailing list to receive RFP's.

- Fundraising campaigns within or outside the organization. List your fund-raising activities.

- Make sure your proposal is within the allowable page limit stated in the RFP or grant application. Preferably use 1-inch margins and size 12 font or follow instructions given by the funder in the RFP or grant application.

- Use the correct margins and font size stated in the RFP or grant application

- Assemble your grant proposal using the instructions in the RFP checklist provided by the funder if a check list has been provided. Follow the instructions perfectly. Don't take shortcuts or deviate from the guideline rules of the application

- Mail or hand deliver your proposal on time. Get a receipt from the funder showing proof of delivery of your application if you hand delivered the application. Send by certified mail if the application is mailed. Put the certified mail receipt in a safe place with a copy of your proposal.

- Use partnerships and collaborate with other agencies and organizations. This strengthens your proposal. Identify and collaborate with key people. These are individuals that you can count on to get the job done.

- Letters of support or commitment- Get letters from key people in your community. Get letters from other organizations, local government agencies, testimonials from past program recipients.

The organization that wins the grant award will be notified by letter. Also, the organization that was denied funding will also be notified by letter. This process is out of your control.

Appeal Process- When an organization is denied funding but they feel they should have been awarded the grant instead of another agency, the organization that was denied can challenge the validity of the grant awarding process. They can ask for the scores of the rating sheets of other competitors and file an appeal if there is just cause. An appeal involves legal representation on both sides and can turn into a lengthy process. The awarded agency will not get the funds until the "appeal process "is over. The funder still has the final determination of who will be awarded the funds.

Do's and Don'ts for writing grant proposals:

Do's for writing a successful proposal:

- Write your grant proposal with clarity
- Know the demographics
- Know the age range, the ethnicity,
- Know the geographical area you want to serve
- State in your proposal that your vision and mission matches that of the funder
- Make sure your vision is clear to the funder
- State your mission with clarity
- State your goals and objectives with clarity
- State the purpose, discuss the achievements and benefits of the program or project
- Be prepared to answer questions of a funder
- Have two or three other people review your proposal critically
- Be willing to accept constructive criticism
- Make the necessary changes to enhance your proposal

- Have a clear definition of your organizations program objectives
- Find out the date the proposal is due to the funder
- Write the proposal with the highest quality possible
- The proposal should be an easy read for the funder
- Check the proposal for grammatical errors and make necessary corrections
- Conduct research for the proposal, research the problem you want to address, and collect data

Don'ts

- Avoid jargon language, avoid street slang words
- Don't use any form of profanity, this can be offensive
- Don't write run on sentences
- Don't make confusing statements
- Don't use complicated sentence structure
- Don't use ambiguous language, be clear in what you want to convey to the reader

Do's

- Make sure you have followed all of the guidelines in the RFP or grant application
- Include all necessary documents or attachments required
- Make sure all of the certifications are signed by the appropriate people
- Make sure the proposal covers the following, your purpose, goals and objectives, vision and mission statements, state the need, activities, staffing, organization, management oversight, timing, accountability, fiscal financial management, and budget request.
- Call funders, have your organization put on the mailing list to receive RFP's
- Complete your proposal and submit to the funder on or before the deadline date and time it is due. The hour it is due will be in the RFP.
- Mail the proposal by certified mail from the US postal service, get proof of mailing

Don'ts

- Don't submit an incomplete proposal to a funder, it will be rejected for funding

- Do not submit your proposal late or past the due date to the funder, if late it will be rejected unless an extension is granted by the funder

Do's

- Submit your proposal in the format and content set forth in the RFP or grant application

- Make sure your proposal request matches the same interest as the funder

- Make sure your proposal is responding to a real need in the community

- Include letters of endorsement for your project, get letters of support from community people such as residents, local businesses, clergy, or other organizations that are familiar with your organization

- Get support letters for your proposal from community leaders, Mayor, Commissioners

- Get support letters from government agencies such as federal, city, state, and county

- Know your politicians, senators, congressional representatives, mayor, governor, and their districts they serve. Attend community meetings, school board meetings, city council meetings in your proposed community

Don'ts

- Do not compromise quality in the delivery of services

- Don't submit a proposal in a field you are not familiar with

Do's

- Have knowledge of your particular field of interest in the proposal

- Use effective methods, approaches and activities to offer resolutions to the problem being addressed

- Have a thorough understanding of the "real" problem you want to address

- Make sure your organization is capable of carrying out all the activities in your proposal

- Demonstrate familiarity with the problem

- State the qualifications of your staff

- Make sure the staff possess the necessary credentials to carry out the activities of the proposal

- Show the experience and resources of your organization

- Show your organizations prior work history or track record of successful operation
- Be honest about your capability to implement your project
- Demonstrate to the funder that your organization is capable of fulfilling the responsibilities of the proposed project
- Give the funder an example of what your organization has done in the past

Don'ts

- Don't make false statements such as years of operation or track record
- Do not compromise the quality and ability of your staff
- Do not make false statements on reports, personnel records, or time sheets

Do's

- Manage your program efficiently, effectively, honestly, and with integrity
- Make sure you have plans for the administration and organization of program activities
- Have a detailed timetable to implement your project
- Indicate the cost of the problem to the community
- Indicate the kinds of managerial and financial systems and controls that will be employed
- Show how advisory boards and committees will be utilized
- Provide regular reports to the funder on time as required
- Hire a professional accountant to handle bookkeeping responsibilities – preferably a CPA
- If all money in your organization is not used by the end of a funding period, notify the funder of any money in reserve from a project that has been funded

Don'ts

- Do not submit reports to your funders past the due date. Penalties may be imposed of the funder
- Do not hire non-qualified staff to handle accounting responsibilities
- Do not hire staff that is not qualified for a particular position or task. If a job description requires someone to have a teaching credential in a certain field or grade level, do not compromise by hiring someone who is not properly credentialed.

If you need a school counselor, make sure the person has a degree in academic counseling.

Do's

- Be realistic about your proposed project

- Make sure you can deliver the goals and objectives of your program activities that you promised in your proposal

- Make sure you can realistically serve the number of people in your proposal

- Show the organizations level of commitment to the proposed project or program

- Make sure you have the resources needed to deliver the services and activities proposed

- The dollar amount requested should be available from the funder

- Get started immediately once you receive the RFP so you will have enough time to write a winning proposal

Don'ts

- Don't be unrealistic with your goals and objectives of your program

- Don't take on more than you can realistically handle involving clients, students, or program participants

- Do not submit a proposal seeking more money than is being offered in the RFP

- Stay within the money allotted for the funding cycle

- Don't write a proposal begging for money, be humble

- Don't complain in your proposal, remain positive

- Do not submit a proposal if the interest does not correspond with the RFP. Example, if the RFP is seeking proposals for an after school tutorial program for youth ages 5-11, but your proposal addresses teen pregnancy prevention and unwed mothers, you would not submit your proposal for this RFP.

- Do not procrastinate when writing the grant proposal. You will run the risk of running out of time to write a winning proposal.

Rating a Proposal – Proposals are assigned points for each component. A review team will rate the proposal by certain criteria using a "rubric score" form. This form is provided by the funding agency. Each proposal submitted will be given a score from 0-100 points. The proposal that receives the highest number of points is usually the agency or organization that will be recommended for funding. The organization that is selected to be granted the funding award will be notified by an official letter from the funder.

Examples of rating criteria:

1. Evidence of community involvement. How will the community be involved in the program or project?

2. How much will the project cost? Is the cost reasonable and feasible?

3. Goals, objectives, mission statements. Are these elements made clear to the funder?

4. Needs assessment. What process was used to determine the need of the people?

5. Collaboration with other agencies/ private sector organizations or businesses

6. Ability of applicant to administer the program or project

7. Fiscal accountability and responsibility

8. Address significance of the problem. Is the "Real Problem" made clear in the proposal?

9. Supporting documentation, support letters for the programs or projects

10. Attachments –legal certification-are all certifications signed by appropriate individuals?

11. Documented need/ need survey results- are the results included in the proposal?

12. Is there duplication and overlapping of services?

13. Methods of evaluating the success of the project. Is the evaluation process clear?

14. Project sustainability- what is the strategy to continue the project when funding ends?

15. Can the project be replicated in other cities, states, and counties?

16. Qualification of staff –Employees, consultants, & subcontractors. Bios are included

17. Who has endorsed this project? Are there letters of support from community residents, business sector, school district, religious community, and political arena- civic leaders, and law enforcement agencies, city, county, state, and federal government officials?

18. The final proposal has all of the necessary required legal signatures. The authorized and appropriate signatures have all been obtained

The funder along with the grant proposal review team looks closely for the answers to all of these criteria. The grant writer must check the finished application very closely to make sure everything that is required in the RFP application has been met to the funder's satisfaction.

Make sure the proposal is free of any mistakes or errors. Check for accuracy and validity of all information in the grant proposal. One missing piece of information can make the difference in the scoring criteria process. Something as simple as a missed signature on a document such as a certification can affect the scoring on a proposal.

The grant writer needs to make sure the proposal has been proofed and edited by a experienced grant writer to make sure that the proposal meets all of the requirements before submitting the final proposal to the funding agency. Grant proposals are very competitive. So you want to make sure the application for your organization is complete. You want the highest score possible.

Chapter 1 Practice worksheet- Fill in the blanks for your organization

Name of Organization: _____

Is there a former name of this organization? Yes ____ or No _____ If yes, Give former name of organization: _____

Location of Address: _____

How long at this address? _____

History of organization: Date it was founded: _____

Has your organization applied for the IRS tax exempt 501(c)(3) application?
Yes ___ No ___

Legal Status: Nonprofit organization 501(c)(3) Has your organization received their "Determination Letter" from the USA Internal Revenue Service?
Yes ___ No _____

Date organization became incorporated: _____

Is this a brand new organization? Yes _____ No _____

What is the Vision of the organization? _____
_____
_____

What is the Mission of the organization? _____
_____
_____

What is the name of your project or program (s)?

_____
_____
_____
_____
_____

What are the goals of your program or project? _____
_____
_____
_____

What are the objectives? _____
_____
_____
_____
_____

What is the purpose of the organization?

_____
_____
_____
_____
_____

Worksheet for needs statement

Tell the funder why you need the money for your project or program. Back up your need with research documentation. For example, survey results, other records or reports from various resources. Focus on the needs of the people you want to serve. Refer to your needs surveys.

Summary of Need Statement: _____
_____
_____
_____
_____
_____
_____
_____
_____
_____
_____
_____
_____
_____

List Organizations Accomplishments: Give dates of accomplishments.

_____
_____
_____
_____
_____
_____
_____
_____
_____
_____
_____
_____
_____

Did the organization get approval from the board of directors to apply for this funding? Yes _____ No _____, If yes, give the date of approval: _____
_____
_____
_____
_____
_____

Advisory Board Members- Does this organization have an advisory board?

Yes _____ No _____ List names: _____
_____
_____
_____
_____
_____

STAFFING PATTERN NEEDS: Fill in the blank- Practice work sheet

Numbers of employees needed for the program or project:_____

Number of Full-time Employees/staff _____

Number of Part-time Employees/staff _____

Staff Qualifications for each position: For example: teacher, counselor, nurse, social worker. The staffing pattern needs to compliment the proposed program activities.

Will consultants be utilized on the project? If so, List their titles and positions.

State if the employee is full-time or part-time. (F/T) or (P/T). Example: Sally X. teacher-F/T
_____
_____
_____
_____
_____

Will volunteers be involved in the program or project? Check one. Yes ___, or No _____, If yes, explain what the volunteer's role will be. What will they be responsible for?

How many volunteers will be needed for the program or project?_____

What will the volunteers do for the organization? List Duties _____
_____
_____
_____
_____

What days of the week will volunteers work?

Monday   How Many Hours _____?

Tuesday   How Many Hours _____?

Wednesday   How Many Hours _____?

Thursday   How Many Hours _____?

Friday   How Many Hours _____?

Saturday   How Many Hours _____?

Sunday   How Many Hours _____?

State how many hours per week that volunteers will be needed on your project or program.

What are the hours of work for the volunteers?

From: _____ a.m.   To: _____ a.m.

From: _____ p.m.   To: _____ p.m.

Total number of volunteer hours per week: _____

Will consultants be used for the program or project? Check one: Yes _____ or No _____

Consultant hours on the proposed project: _____

How many days per week? _____

What are the organizations core values? _____
_____
_____
_____
_____
_____

What is the philosophy of the organization?
_____
_____
_____

_____
_____
_____

Why was the organization started?

_____
_____
_____
_____
_____
_____

What are the demographics? Circle all that apply

Who do you plan to serve? Example: Male, female, elderly, adults, children, teens, infants, families.

Number of individuals to be served:_____

Number of families to be served:_____

Number of children to be served:_____ ,

Number of elderly to be served_____

What age group (s) will you serve?_____

Is there any particular ethnic group or culture to be served? If yes, Explain the reason _____
_____
_____
_____
_____
_____

What is unique about your organization's program or project for which you are seeking funding? _____
_____
_____
_____

Who else is doing the same or similar program or project in your proposed area? Name the organization or business _____
_____
_____

Would your program or project be considered a duplication of services? Yes _____ No ____

Is there another agency doing the same kind of program or project that you are proposing in the same geographical area? Yes ____ or No _____ If yes, would you be willing to partner with this other agency? How would your organization coordinate services to support each other? Explain the plan of combined effort. If no, explain why not.

_____
_____
_____
_____
_____

Name other organizations you can collaborate with: _____
_____
_____
_____
_____

Would your program or project be considered a duplication of services? Yes____ No._____
_____
_____

What is the real problem you are addressing? What does the community or people need? __
_____
_____
_____
_____

What method did you use to determine the need for your program or project? _____
_____
_____
_____
_____

Did you conduct a needs assessment of the community? Yes___ No ___, If yes, Give the date of last needs assessment of this community. _____
_____
_____
_____

In what community did you conduct the needs assessment? Name the community or area.
_____
_____
_____

If your organization has not conducted a needs assessment yet, when will it be done? Give date.
_____
_____
_____

What members of the community support your program or project? List names of community leaders.:
_____
_____
_____
_____

List names of organizations that support your proposed program or project:
_____
_____
_____
_____

List political/civic leaders that support your program or project:

_____
_____
_____
_____
_____

List the business owners that support your program or project:

_____
_____
_____
_____
_____

List the churches that support your program or project:

_____
_____
_____
_____
_____

How would your program or project improve the community? Refer to your goals and objectives.

_____
_____
_____
_____
_____

What can your organization do to improve the situation? State the method

_____
_____
_____
_____
_____

How will you measure the success of your program or project? Evaluation Plan: Explain your method of evaluation process:

How will your program or project be funded in the future when the funding ends? Discuss in detail the sustainability of the project or program being proposed.

Name possible funders you will rely on to sustain your program or project: This can be government funding, private sector donations, fundraisers, public or private foundations, corporate gifts, and in-kind contributions. Discuss the contribution the funder has committed to sustain funding to your project or program.

SWOT ANALYSIS ASSESSMENTS- A FUNDING PLAN

Developing a funding plan requires the grant writer to be proactive for your organization. This can be a team effort where other participants are involved in the process also. The team can brainstorm and come up with some creative ideas. A swot analysis assessment can be very helpful when an organization is in the process of seeking funding for their programs or services. What is a SWOT ANALYSIS? "A SWOT analysis is essential for formulating new business strategies. It combines an internal analysis of strengths and weaknesses, with an external environment analysis of opportunities and threats" (Price, R. W. 2004)

All programs and projects require a funding plan. This means conducting an assessment of funding needs. In order to come up with an assessment plan that is proactive and realistic, the grant writer should conduct a SWOT analysis.

In the private business sector, a (SWOT) analysis is done to assess the organization's internal and external environments. S=strength, W=weakness, O=opportunities, T=threats. A SWOT analysis is a good tool to use when you want to look at your organization with a critical eye to determine its strengths, weaknesses, opportunities, and threats. It's an extensive and complete examination of how your organization functions from the inside out. A SWOT analysis can also be utilized in nonprofit organizations when you are developing a funding plan for your program or project. A "SWOT" analysis is not only done to assess private business plans, but can also be applied to social service agencies, educational institutions, medical institutions, religious groups and churches. This kind of critical analysis will give the grant seeker valuable information which will help to develop an effective funding plan for your program or project for your nonprofit organization.

Strengths:

What are the strengths? Ask the following questions when you are assessing your needs for funding. What are all of the positive **strengths** of your organization? The organization's strengths represent your internal environment assets. What funding sources will be made available to your organization long term beyond three years? Who can you count on for continued funding for your programs or projects? What are the positive aspects of your organization? What does your organization do well? What programs or services has the organization provided to your target population that proved to be a positive benefit to the clients and or the community? Does the organization have a grant writer that can write grant applications with a high success rate of getting funded? What is the percentage of funding that the organization has received in the past? Who is responsible for writing the grant applications? Does this person have the experience and qualifications to seek funding for the organization? Does the organization's programs and services receive high visibility in the communities it serves? These are just scenarios of questions to assist you with assessing your organizations strengths. Look at your organizations current programs and services and list the strengths that your organization possess.

Weaknesses:

What are the weaknesses? Look at your organization and asses its weaknesses. The weaknesses are areas that are negative to the organization. The weakness represents your organization's external liabilities. What are the **weaknesses** of your organization? Example, there is not enough staffing. What are the gaps in services in your organization? Does the organization lack finances? Some of the weaknesses might be that the organization may have difficulties collecting relative data such as evaluation data, conducting and analyzing survey results from program participants who have received services from the organization in the past, goals and objectives were not met in previous grant applications, or does the organization have difficulties in getting funding for lack of communication with previous funders? One of the main responsibilities of board members is to identify funding for the organization. Do the board members assist with fundraising activities to help raise funding for the organizations? Many board members are very influential in the community. They are usually well connected to businesses in the community. Board members can assist with obtaining funding from government sources, private foundations, corporations, as well as individuals. If board members do not help with obtaining funding for the organization, this can be a serious weakness for the organization and can negatively impact the organizations ability to obtain funding. List the weaknesses that exist in your organization. I have only given scenarios of weaknesses that may exist. Think about weaknesses in your own organization.

Opportunities:

What are the opportunities that the organization can have as a result of the funding? Example, identify new funders. Ask the following questions. Who can provide funding for your programs or project? Has your organization contacted your local government agencies? Have you considered looking to the Federal, State, City, or County governments for possible funding for your programs? Does the organization's staff meet and collaborate with other social-service organizations to discuss possible funding opportunities? Is the organization on multiple mailing lists to grant making organizations and agencies? Does the organization subscribe to newsletters, magazines, bulletins, or other written materials that will inform the organization of any funding opportunities? Does the organization know the funding cycles for government or foundation funding? Does the organization have a champion that can bring funding to the organization?

List the opportunities you have researched that will assure your organization of funding for the next three to five years. You may know of other opportunities I have not mentioned here. These are just scenarios to think about.

Threats:

What are the threats? Example, what would happen if the funding is not provided or if the funding ends? Competitors or competition can be a real threat to your organizations funding. Ask the following questions when you are assessing the threats of your organization. Has the organization received any negative publicity in the public view? Negative publicity in the news media can have a very serious impact on future funding of an organization. If funding is coming to an end on a current program, how will the organization continue to function without new or continued funding? How will your program be impacted with the reduction or loss of funding? Are your competitors hurting your efforts in any way that prevents your organization from being funded? Are there any elected local politicians against your program initiatives? If so, how will they influence or impact your organizations funding? Do they have the power to block funding to your organization? If so, how will your organization handle this threat?

List the threats to your organizations funding. They can be different from what I have stated here. These are just scenarios to think about.

Applaud the positive aspects of your organization and continue to strive towards excellence in the planning and delivery of your programs or projects. When you identify the weaknesses and threats in the organization this is the time to come up with a strategic action plan to address these problems. When you have completed your "SWOT" analysis for your organization, you will be able to develop your program or project with clear direction. You will put the organization on the right path to success.

Practice worksheet for "SWOT ANALYSIS":

List the strengths of your organization: Internal Environment _____
_____
_____
_____
_____
_____
_____
_____
_____
_____
_____
_____
_____
_____
_____
_____

Weaknesses: _____
_____
_____
_____
_____
_____
_____

OPPORTUNITIES: External Environment _____

SWOT ANALYSIS: External Environment

THREATS: _____

What is your "Action Plan" to address the issues of weaknesses and threats to your organization?

___

NOTES: Chapter 1

Date: _____

Things I need to do: _____
_____
_____
_____
_____
_____
_____
_____

Notes:
_____
_____
_____
_____
_____
_____
_____
_____
_____
_____
_____
_____
_____
_____
_____
_____
_____
_____
_____
_____
_____
_____
_____
_____
_____

Chapter 2:
Goals and Objectives

Goals-Your goal should be related to the stated need. A goal addresses the ultimate change you want to undertake. A goal can be short-term or long term. Example of a goal is to decrease crime rate in a community.

"A goal should be realistic and achievable." Goals are statements of the major steps to accomplish the mission of the project Cheryl C. New and James A. Quick explain that goals have five parts. What you are going to do, what approach you will use, when you are going to do it, for how many/how much, and what result is desired. (New, C & Quick, J.1998)

Objective- An objective is measurable. It has a specific time that the organization expects to see a result as proposed in the project. Objectives are also known as "outcomes". The objective gives the method of how the project will accomplish its goal. The objective will state an impact or the result. What will be the impact of your proposed project or program? The objectives require specific statements of what will be accomplished. (Lefferts, R. 2nd edition 1982).

3 steps in an objective

1. The measurement or evaluation of the project

2. The result you hope to accomplish

3. The timeframe – how long the project will take? When will the result happen? When will the project be accomplished or finished?

Objectives should be stated as to the "outcome". Objectives should identify the population group being served. Objectives should be capable and realistic of being accomplished within a timeframe. Your objectives should state what change your organization wants to make. When, where, and who will be involved and the degree of change to increase or decrease. What is the deadline for the change? Include time line.

Example of an objective

The purpose of this program is to reduce the crime rate in the community. There will be a 10% decrease in crime due to a new crime prevention program that will be established and implemented in the community. The crime prevention program will be evaluated by conducting a survey at the end of the first year of operation which will be by June 31, 2010.

Writing goals and objectives

- Goals and objectives must relate to the need statement
- State your target population
- Develop a reasonable timeframe to carry out and accomplish your objectives
- Include your expected result

Key words for objectives statement

Direction for change for programs: Explain the purpose for the change in your objective.

- To reduce
- To expand
- To increase
- Target population- persons to be served
- Degree of change- state by percentage, for example, crime will decrease by 10%
- Time-frame – Duration of time of project. How long will it take to accomplish the result, for example, 2 months, 6 months, 1 year
- To facilitate
- To improve
- To make
- To identify

Chapter 2: Practice Worksheet Goals and Objectives

List the goals for your organization's proposal: Long term or short term

Short Term Goals:

1. _____

2. _____

3. _____

Long Term Goals:

1. _____

2. _____

3. _____

List objectives for your organization's proposal

Be specific about the methods of how you are going to accomplish your goals

1. _____

2. _____

3. _____

4. _____

5. _____

NOTES: Chapter 2

Date: _____

Things I need to do: _____

Notes:

Chapter 3:
Letter of Intent to Apply for Funding

The letter of intent is a formal letter that is addressed to the organization of the funder. The letter must be written on official letterhead stationery of the organization. The stationery should include the name and address of the organization along with the telephone number. If the organization is incorporated let the funder know this information. The board of director's names should also be listed on the letterhead stationery.

The letter should give a detailed summary of the problem that you want to address. Make sure you state the purpose for the proposed project. The goals and objectives should be clearly stated as well as the proposed program approach. Also, give a brief statement of the development of your program plan.

The intent letter should be addressed to the correct individual. The RFP will usually give the full name of the person that should receive the letter. If the RFP does not give the name of the person who should receive the letter, the grant writer can call the funder and ask who the letter of intent should be addressed to. Make sure the person's name is spelled correctly. Don't guess at the spelling of the name. Many names sound the same but may be spelled differently. For example, the name Gail can also be spelled Gayle.

The letter of intent should also state the organizations interest in the project which is referenced in the RFP. State the name or title of your proposed project or program. Also give the number of the project that is listed on the grant application. Date the letter. The organization also should state the experience and capability to develop and implement the project or program. Be sure to describe your proposed project adequately and effectively with clarity.

Discuss what you hope to accomplish from your proposed project. Also discuss the methods you will use to accomplish your goals. State the name and address of a contact person of your organization in case the funder needs any further information. Address the individual in a formal context for example, Mr., Mrs., Miss, Ms., or Dr. Give the title of the position the contact person holds. Avoid first name only, even if you know the individual on a personal basis. Keep the letter professional.

The letter of intent can also serve as a letter of transmittal. This letter should be one page but do not exceed two pages. This letter serves as an introduction to your organization which will give the funder some idea of whom and what your organization wants to do for a target population or community. The letter should show how your organization shares the same interest as the funder. Remember to only submit a letter of intent to a funder if your organization can convince the funder that your proposed program or project matches their interest for funding.

If you know your organization is not a match to the funders interest do not submit the proposal for funding. Your organization may have another opportunity to submit a proposal at a future time.

The reason for the letter of intent to the funder is to give the funder a better understanding of the number of entities that intend to apply for funding. While it is not mandatory to send a letter of intent to apply for funding, it is strongly recommended by the funder that each potential applicant send a notification of its intent to apply for the funding in the grant announcement.

SAMPLE of LETTER of INTENT

Senior Citizen Substance Abuse Prevention Program
Date 4-12-2010 RE: Grant announcement number GASS 100.00

Ms. Janice Doe, Executive Director
Blue Sky Foundation, Inc.
30 Green Waye St.
Proposal Ville, MN USA 90000

Dear Ms. Doe,

The XYZ organization is pleased to submit the enclosed proposal to provide a substance abuse prevention program to senior citizens of Blue County. This program is in keeping with the expressed goal of your foundation to support older adults. The purpose of the program is to demonstrate the effectiveness of providing a range of health educational classes that will prevent substance abuse among senior citizens. The program is endorsed by the county health department.

We believe that by providing educational awareness in the area of substance abuse to the elderly population as well as providing much needed social services, there would be a decrease in the incidence of unnecessary emergency room admissions.

The XYZ organization has provided an array of social services to individuals 55 and over in Blue County since 1970. As an incorporated non-profit agency we have demonstrated in the past 33 years of operation that we have the capability and experience to successfully carry out similar programs and services for the aged. We have highly skilled, capable and qualified staff that has years of experience in operating community based programs.

Our Board of Directors consists of men and women of diverse backgrounds and all are highly committed to this organization. They represent the major interests of our community and have many years of experience in establishing policies to assure efficiency and effectiveness of the organizations operations.

The enclosed proposal outlines in detail the goals, objectives, services to be rendered or provided, staffing, management plan, and budget for this proposed program. We would be glad to discuss this proposal with you at your convenience and are willing to provide any further information you may want. We are looking forward to hearing from you.

Sincerely,

Kattie XX, President

Worksheet – Questions for Practice Letter of Intent

Your organizations letter of intent can serve both as a relationship builder and a source of background information on your proposed project. Your letter of intent should include the following:

1. Purpose of program
2. Your organization's mission statement and related programs
3. The need your organization wishes to meet
4. The outcome expected by your organization's project
5. Details of how your organization will conduct the project
6. State how your organization's proposed project fits the funders interest
7. State the program or project objectives

Letter of Intent Questionnaire

1. Does your project or program fit with the funder? Yes _____ No _____

2. Whom is the letter being sent to? _____

3. Give history of the organization. What year was the organization founded?
_____

4. Give year when the organization was incorporated? _____

5. What are the long term goals of your organization?
_____
_____
_____
_____

6. What are your objectives? _____
_____
_____
_____
_____

7. What programs support your goals in your organization? _____
_____
_____
_____
_____
_____

8. What is the need in your community for seeking funding? _____
_____
_____
_____
_____
_____
_____

9. What do you propose to do to meet the need?

_____
_____
_____
_____
_____
_____
_____
_____
_____
_____
_____

10. What is your expected outcome after the first year of funding?

_____
_____
_____
_____
_____
_____
_____
_____
_____
_____
_____

11. How many years do you want funding for? _____

12. How much money are you asking the funder for? State cost per year?

$_____ Cost per year

Total amount of money = cost x number of years. $_____

13. Who will be the designated contact person for your organization to determine its interest?

_____
_____

14. Who will be in direct contact with the funder to get Request for proposals?

_____
_____
_____
_____
_____

15. Name the person or persons who will have direct contact with the funder through oral or written communication: No more than two people. Give title of person(s).

_____ title of person: _____
_____ title of person: _____

There should be no more than 2 people listed as contact people for the organization. These two people are usually the agency administrator and the department head of a particular department within the organization. However, these people can be anyone selected by the authority of the organization. It can be the CEO of the organization or a board member. Every organization is different with individuals participating in different roles.

Practice Worksheet: Chapter 3: Letter of Intent

Date: _____

Contact person: _____

Organization Name: _____

Address: City _____

State _____

Zip _____

Dear: _____
_____
_____
_____
_____
_____
_____
_____
_____
_____
_____
_____
_____
_____
_____
_____
_____
_____
_____
_____
_____
_____
_____
_____
_____
_____

NOTES: Chapter 3

Date: _____

Things I need to do: _____

Notes:

Chapter 4:
Statement of Need

Writing a need statement is essential and a very important component of the proposal. A funder wants to make sure your need addresses the problem for a community. Funders must feel that your organization's project is an important need. Your need statement must be compelling enough to get the attention of the funder. The need statement must be very strong in order to rally the support of a funder. If the need statement is weak, the funder has no reason to continue to read the rest of your proposal. The need statement must be clear and concise. There must be strong evidence that the problem addressed is a real need for the community. The need statement should describe the condition of a specific problem or social need affecting a specific group of people or to fill a void in a certain community.

The need statement should provide the following:

1. Provide a clear relationship to the organization's mission and purpose
2. Focus on the need of whom your organization serves
3. Need should be documented with evidence of facts such as statistical data, expert testimony, research, and community input if applicable
4. Your organization's ability to respond to the need in your proposal

Justify the need statement

- Use statistical data, true numbers to support your need
- State the scope of the problem
- Support your argument with clear statistics
- Show evidence of the problem. Include research evidence

- Site quotes from researchers and other authorities on the topic you are addressing

- Have strong documentation

- Surveys

- Obtain testimonials of people your organization has helped

- Mention the need the people or community has, not a wish list

- State the source for research data

- State the urgency for your project. What will happen if your organization is not funded?

- Show need for demographical area. Describe the people or community in need.

- Explain the need on the geographical area to be served

- State the positive impact the funding will have when a problem is resolved, eliminated or reduced.

- State truthful and honest facts about the problem and need

- Avoid using false numbers

- Avoid using untrue statements. Don't use misleading statements

- Don't use false documentation

Sample Need Statement for Counseling Center for Teens

Eighty five percent (85%) of the population of Dolby County are teenagers ranging in ages from 13 – 17. Fifty five percent (55%) of teenagers run away from home each year. The Department of Family Services recently conducted a survey among teenagers to find out what they needed most to enhance their lives and provide a comfortable home environment. The highest priority for the teens according to the survey was to have a counseling center in their community where they could go to talk to someone when things got tough at home.

The county has many social services and recreational activities available to teenagers such as after school programs, arts programs, drama, music, and dance. However, due to the lack of funding, the county does not have any additional funds for a counseling program. Therefore, when teenagers are in trouble they feel they have no one else to turn to but the lonely dark streets. Some teenagers live in abusive households where they are constantly subjected to obscene language, physical and mental abuse, alcoholism of parents, substance abuse and lack of respect. There has been a thirty (30%) reduction of staffing by the county due to loss of county funding, therefore counseling is not available anywhere in this county.

Due to the fact that many troubled teenagers resort to leaving home and choose to live their lives on the streets, they often end up getting into trouble and consequently end up in the juvenile justice system. This agency is in desperate need of a counseling center for teenagers at risk of getting involved with drugs, gangs, robberies, assaults and other criminal activity because they are hurting and need to feel a sense of comfort and safety. Without the financial support that is needed to prevent our teenagers from getting into trouble, society as a whole will pay the price through the correctional systems of the county.

As a result of funding, a county wide counseling center can be established. The counseling center would reduce the number of teenagers running away from home because they will now have some place to turn to when they need help and support in a time of crisis. The counseling center would be community based and would provide counseling by professionally trained staff who have expertise in the area of adolescent counseling.

Chapter 4 Practice Worksheet– Need Statement

1) Name of Organization: _____

2) Population: Who is in need? _____

3) Where does the problem exist? _____

4) Name the community or area – Geographical or catchment area to be served

_____
_____
_____
_____
_____

5) Does the need problem affect a specific ethnic or cultural group? Yes ___ No _____

If so, what group?

_____
_____
_____
_____
_____

6) Why do you feel this group is in need?

_____
_____
_____
_____
_____

7) What age group is in need or at risk for this problem?

_____
_____
_____
_____
_____

8) When did the real problem become evident?

9) Why is this group of people at risk more than other groups? Show evidence:

10) What evidence or proof do you have to support your statement of need?

11) Is there another agency or organization in your community that is meeting the same need or addressing the same problem that you are proposing? Yes _____ or No _____

If yes, name the organization:

12) Describe how your organization goals & mission relates to the need or problem. _____

13) How will the community be informed of your program, services, or project? _____

14) Describe the nature, size, and scope of the need to be addressed.

15) How critical is the need for your project or program?

16) What would be the consequence if your agency does not get funded to address the stated need or problem of your project, programs, or services?

NOTES: Chapter 4

Date: _____

Things I need to do: _____

Notes:

Chapter 5:
Establishing Relationships with Funder

Government agencies and foundations are clear about what they want to fund. Annual reports and grant guidelines are established for public review. Some funders make this information available on their websites.

Materials to ask for:

1. Annual reports
2. Grant Guidelines
3. An application form
4. Deadlines for receiving proposals

Grant seekers should develop a list of the funder's priorities that seem applicable to the organizations proposal. While writing the proposal, the grant writer should clearly spell out the parts of the project, or programs that fit those priorities. Building a good relationship with a funder is a continuous process. The relationship can span over many years. Even after the funding has stopped the funder likes to hear of the on-going progress of a program that they initially funded. A funder may want to fund another project that the organization has developed. Invite the funder for a tour of your program or project and make their visit comfortable. Show the funder how appreciative you are to them for their financial support.

Strategies for meeting a funder

Telephone conversations with funders can establish relationships. The person you speak with may have a very short time to listen to your proposal idea by telephone. Think about what you want to say. Keep it brief but thorough enough to give the funder a clear idea of what you are proposing to do. Answer all questions asked. Listen closely to the funders needs and provide the information the funder wants. Do not assume anything. Giving the funder exactly what they ask for is extremely important. You will begin to build a relationship with the funder even before they see your letter of intent through your telephone conversation.

1. Be a part of community interest groups, businesses, churches. Become active in civic groups.

2. Join advisory committees – attend meetings

3. Attend school board meetings regularly- get to know all school board members by name

4. Attend city council meetings – get to know all council members

5. Get involved with civic organizations

6. Get to know your elected government officials, i.e. senators, congressional representative and their districts, mayor, and governor.

7. Invite a funder to your facility to observe your current programs in operation

8. Provide your funder with brochures and literature about your organization

9. Invite your funder to lunch to begin to establish a business relationship

You may meet a funder in anyone of these settings. Get to know key people in the private business sector as well as governmental agencies. Get involved – attend meetings. Get to know the movers and shakers.

Once you meet key people that have influence, you can set up a meeting to discuss your proposal. In this meeting you want to discuss your organization. Give some background information. Discuss its credibility. Give a description of your project or program. Discuss the need for your project. Discuss the community's interest in your project. What is your expected outcome and how will you measure the success of the project? Discuss the proposed cost. Who and how will the project be managed for efficiency and effectiveness? Be prepared to answer any questions the funder may have. Answer all questions truthfully and honestly. Make sure your project is a good fit for the funder.

NOTES: Chapter 5

Date: _____

Things I need to do: _____

Notes:

Chapter 6:
Method Component

A method describes how your organization will conduct its activities or strategies. The method will tell the funder how the organization will implement the activities to achieve its objectives. The proposal should describe your program staffing. It should also identify the population you wish to serve and justify why you selected that population.

The Methods component should include the following:

1. Activities or strategies of the project

2. The budget – what's on hand? (money available)?

3. Staffing pattern (personnel that is available)

4. Starting and ending dates of the project, i.e. time-line

5. Responsibility –who is responsible for the project completion?

6. Who are the participants? i.e., clients

7. How will the participants be selected for your program or project?

8. Are there any eligibility requirements or criteria for people to participate in the program? Example, income requirements, low-income individuals, single moms, unemployed people, disabled persons, elderly or senior citizen.

9. Are there criteria to participate in the program? Yes____No___. If yes, what is the criteria to participate?

10. What is the methodology?

11. How will the problem be corrected or resolved?

12. What will be your approach to change the situation?

Practice worksheet: Chapter 6: Timeline

Several proposals have many different activities and must be implemented in phases, which means you will have to establish a reasonable timeline to accomplish the activities within the timeframe stated in your proposal. If the funding period spans over a 12 month period you will need to develop a timeline calendar to make sure you can begin your project on time and carry out the activities over a 12 month period with a good degree of efficiency.

Using a 12 month timeline, develop a calendar of activities that will be completed by the end of the 12 month. Listed are areas that will need attention for a brand new project.

Example:

Month – January – December

	Jan	Feb	Mar	Apr	May	Jun	Jul	Aug	Sept	Oct	Nov	Dec
Activity	1	2	3	4	5	6	7	8	9	10	11	12

1. Advertise positions
2. Hire new staff, training
3. Develop objectives for specific programs, tasks,
4. Identify children who need child care
5. Design outreach strategies for the community
6. Begin to develop childcare program curriculum
7. Implement childcare program
8. Evaluate program at 2 month, 5 month, and 12 month intervals

Writing the methods component consist of the following:

1. Methods should tie to the needs statement
2. Show rationale for why you chose the method for your project, i.e. research findings, your organizations experiences, expert opinions, your past experience with similar programs
3. List facilities and capital equipment that are available for the project
4. Develop a reasonable timeline
5. Clarify who will be served. How will the participants be selected for the program or project?

6. Provide the funder with a clear picture of the steps your organization will take to accomplish its goals and objectives.

7. Give specific details of all of your planned activities for your program or project. Government agencies may require detailed information than other funders.

Chapter 6 Practice Worksheet: Methods Component

List tasks to be performed

_____
_____
_____
_____
_____

Who is responsible for what tasks? List person(s)

_____
_____
_____
_____
_____

What resources will you need for your program or project, i.e. equipment, supplies or materials?

List: _____
_____
_____
_____
_____

What resources do you already have?

List: _____
_____
_____
_____
_____

Will your project or program need transportation vehicles? Yes ___ or No _____

If yes, what type of vehicle, i.e. bus or van? _____

How will the vehicle be used? Explain _____
_____
_____
_____

What is your projected start date? Give date: _____

When is your completion date? Give date: _____

Example for methods component

<u>Tasks</u>

Advertise positions

Hire new staff

Develop child care program for pre-school children

Who is responsible? <u>Director of human resources</u>

What resources will you need? Staff/personnel, budget for salaries, sleeping folding beds, tables, chairs, food and toys.

What resources do you already have? <u>Stove, refrigerator, 1 teacher, 1 director</u>

Start date: April 1, 2010 (Example)

Finish date: _____ 2010

Give dates in between as program develops: <u>3 month intervals April 1, 2010 – July 1, 2010</u>

Guidelines for Writing Successful Grant Proposals for Nonprofit Organizations | 71

TIMING:

State each phase and put a timeline to it:

Month – January – December

	Jan	Feb	Mar	Apr	May	Jun	Jul	Aug	Sept	Oct	Nov	Dec
Activity	1	2	3	4	5	6	7	8	9	10	11	12

Advertise positions

Interview new staff/hire new staff, train staff

Develop goals and objectives for specific programs, tasks,

Identify children who need child care

Design outreach strategies for the community-disseminate information

Begin to develop childcare program curriculum

Implement childcare program

Evaluate program at 2 month, 5 month, and 12 month intervals

Fill in the start date. Name the activity. Give the date the activity will end. The activity chart can be as long as you wish. Be realistic for your time frames.

Start Date	Activity	End Date

Write a brief paragraph explaining the timetable for each activity.

_____
_____
_____
_____
_____
_____
_____

NOTES: Chapter 6

Date: _____

Things I need to do: _____

Notes:

Chapter 7:
Evaluation Component

All programs or projects should be evaluated for its efficiency, quality of services provided, and the effectiveness of the program or project which was funded. Success is demonstrated by how the goals and objectives were accomplished. Was the expected outcome achieved? Funders want the reassurance that their money will be well spent for a worthy cause. Organizations should determine the method of evaluation before the project is even implemented.

Funders use a rubric form to evaluate project or programs. This is a score form provided by the funding agency to help readers form an opinion or evaluation of the proposed program or project and how it positions itself against agency's guidelines. (Burke, J. & Prater, C. 2000).

Funders want to know how an agency or organization is going to measure success of a program or project. Evaluation is a very important component of the proposal process. Funders of the proposal want to believe they have made a great investment in trying to bring about a positive change in a community. Be sure to develop a continuation plan for your project. Let the funder know how your program is going to continue whether the project is funded again or not. Include letters of support in your continuation plan. Show strong support and commitment of your organization to ensure that your program or project will continue. Show strong evidence of how your organization has developed and implemented programs or projects in the past.

An evaluation will let an organization know what works or what does not work in a given situation. It will tell if a program or project succeeded or failed. In creating an evaluation design, it must be effective. If the evaluation design is ineffective the organization will not know whether or not their program or project was successful.

Once the organization has gained knowledge from the results of their evaluation they can now share this information with the staff. It can help to improve programs and services. This information can also be shared with other outside agencies and organizations to give them some insight as to the organizations progress. The organization can also make positive changes if the result of the evaluation proves that changes need to be made to make the programs and projects more efficient and effective.

An organization that receives funding is obligated to let the public at large know that programs and projects are succeeding in meeting the goals and objectives that were stated in the proposal. The public can request this information for measuring real success of a program or project.

Steps of the evaluation component

1. Design an evaluation tool that is effective and realistic

2. Define the word "success" as it relates to your organization

3. How does your organization evaluate its programs or projects? Give a lot of thought in designing your evaluation tool

4. Make sure you carried out the activities you proposed for your program or project

5. Make sure the methods used met the objectives of your program or project

6. Get feedback from your program participants (targeted population). This can be done by a simple questionnaire survey. Don't make it too long and complicated. Consider the intellect of your population, age, level of education, and community, etc.

7. Adjust program activities to ensure its success

8. It is important to maintain control over the program or project. Who is responsible for the program or project? Select a key person.

Quantitative Documentation Materials – Use statistical data to stress the need for funding for your program or project. You can include demographics, test scores, survey results, the size and location of where your program or project will be developed and implemented. This kind of documentation will strengthen your need for funding.

Qualitative Documentation – State the problems and discuss factors that will be influenced by the funding. For example, teen pregnancy is on the increase due to lack of health preventive education in the home or in the school system.

Proof and Evidence of Need – Writing your need statement is critical to your entire proposal. Discuss the problem and the need for change. Explain what you are proposing to the community and how you have demonstrated in the past that your organization has the experience and capability to succeed in carrying out the goals and objectives of the programs or project. Previous studies, reports, and newspaper articles can serve as basis to give you information of the problem you are trying to resolve in the community. Use statistics and accurate facts to support your need for the proposed funding. Write a compelling need statement to the funder convincing them that your proposal is going to meet an important need that the target population and community will truly benefit from.

Collecting information and data to evidence need- You must document the need for funding for your grant proposal. There are many ways to convince the funder the need for funding your proposed program or project: Collect various kinds of evidence to support your grant application. This can be done by conducting a needs assessment of the community you are proposing to provide programs and services. Surveys taken by the prospective program participants can give valuable information about the void of services as well as real problems in their communities. Information can be gathered from government agencies, medical reports, hospital records, birth records, health records at clinics and other health departments, statistics, school records, school test results, collect demographic information, cultural and ethnicity information, socioeconomic statistics, university records, stats, law enforcement agencies, public social service agencies, newspaper and magazine articles, current research data, and social service surveys conducted by several different agencies, waiting list established by other social service agencies that cannot accommodate the numbers of people that need services, and referrals from other resources. You may need to do a lot of research in this area. Include research reports and literature to show the funder evidence of the need for funding your project or program. Show the funder that you are familiar with the field you are seeking funding. The funder wants to feel and believe that your organization has the capability and competence to carry out the mission statement as well as the goals and objectives of your proposed program or project. Submitting strong facts of evidence for the need of funding will strengthen the validity of your grant proposal.

Resource Materials – You will need resource materials to prepare your problem statement, your need statement, and rationale for your proposed program or project. Here is a list of resource materials that may help you in gathering very important information.

1. Census reports, population surveys, statistical abstract
2. Reports from governmental agencies, local and state planning agencies
3. Gather annual reports from relevant agencies
4. Surveys done by local and state planning agencies
5. Surveys done by other non-profit agencies
6. Surveys done by schools- public & private, universities, other agencies
7. Literature from governmental agencies
8. Information from private foundations, corporations
9. Reports of legislative committees
10. Published testimony given at public hearings
11. Recently signed presidential initiatives
12. Newspaper articles
13. Magazine articles

14. Surveys done by medical institutions
15. Recent statistics from agencies that collect data for your specific proposed program or project
16. Local libraries
17. Internet and other technology resources

Example of quantitative data results: These are fictitious numbers for illustration purposes only

Target Communities   Race (number)   Race (%)

	Black	White	Asian	Mexican	Black
California	1000	1000	1000	1000	50.0
Detroit	500	4500	500	4500	10.0
South Carolina	2500	500	2500	500	83.0
Total	4000	6000	4000	6000	40.0

Example Evaluation Planning

Questions that can be considered while developing your proposal

1. What kind of information will the organization seek to evaluate its programs?
2. What kind of data will be collected?
3. What kind of instrument will be used to evaluate your programs?
4. What kind of comparison group or baseline will be used?
5. How will you measure the success of your programs or project?
6. Was your program implemented as planned?
7. Who will conduct the evaluation?
8. Who is responsible for reporting the success of your program?
9. How will the organization define its success for your program or project?
10. Does your organization program of activities focus on the mission statement?
11. What are your demographics?
12. What are your test scores?
13. Who is going to manage the program or project?
14. Who is your target group population?

15. Where is the location of your project or program?

16. What criteria will be used to select clients or participants for your program or project?

17. Were the goals and objectives met as proposed?

18. Who will collect and analyze the statistical data?

Practice Worksheet
Chapter 7: fill in the blanks- Evaluation Tool

Questions to be answered by grant writer to develop an evaluation tool

1. Who will be responsible for the design and implementation of the evaluation tool?
   _____
   _____

2. What is the purpose of the evaluation? _____
   _____
   _____

3. Who will participate in the evaluation process? _____
   _____
   _____

4. What will your organization learn from the evaluation results? _____
   _____
   _____
   _____

5. What will be the methods of getting and collecting the data from the participants?
   _____
   _____
   _____

6. Who will have access to the evaluation results? _____
   _____
   _____

7. How will the results be utilized? _____
   _____
   _____

8. Did the organization meet all of the goals and objectives proposed to the funder?
   Yes _____ No _____

9. Were the funds used correctly for the program or project as proposed?
   Yes _____ No _____

10. Did the organization accomplish its expected outcome? Yes _____ No _____

11. Did the program participants receive quality activities and services as stated in the proposal? Yes _____ No _____

12. Who is responsible for making sure that the programs and services are in contract compliance? _____
   _____
   _____

13. Who will analyze the collected data? Give name _____
    _____

14. Did you use both qualitative methods and quantitative methods to collect data?
    Yes _____ No _____

If you did not use both, which evaluation method did you use and why? _____
_____
_____
_____
_____
_____

Practice worksheet–
Chapter 7: Design an evaluation tool

CLIENT EVALUATION SURVEY

Program/Client participant-Client name is optional. Survey is voluntary.

Did this program meet your expectations? Yes _____ No _____ If not, how can it be improved? _____

Is the program meeting your needs? Yes _____ No _____ Explain _____
_____
_____
_____

How has the program helped you? Explain _____
_____
_____
_____

What did you gain most from the program? Explain _____
_____
_____
_____

What did you like most about the program? Explain _____
_____
_____
_____

What did you like least about the program? Explain _____
_____
_____
_____

How did you hear about this program? Explain _____
_____
_____
_____

Who referred you to this program? _____

Was the staff courteous and polite to you? Yes _____ No _____

If this program was not available to you where could you go to receive services? _____
_____
_____
_____
_____
_____
_____

Does this organizations business hours meet your needs? Yes _____ No _____

If no, how can we best meet your needs? Explain _____
_____
_____
_____
_____
_____

Would you recommend this program to people that you know? Yes _____ No _____

13. On a scale of 1-5, 1 being the best, 5 being the worst, how would you rate the services you have received from this program?

Please give the name of the program you participated in:

_____ Date (s) of participation: _____

Name of program participant is optional: _____

Survey scale 1-5. Please circle your level of satisfaction for services you received.

1. Extremely satisfied. The services exceeded my expectations. Outstanding services received.

2. Very satisfied. Met all of my expectations

3. Satisfied. Met most of my expectations

4. Somewhat dissatisfied. Met only some of my expectations

5. Extremely dissatisfied. The program did not meet any of my expectations at all.

Additional Comments: Feel free to tell us what you think about our programs._____
_____
_____
_____
_____
_____
_____
_____
_____
_____
_____
_____
_____
_____
_____
_____
_____

Name optional: Signature _____

Telephone number: Optional _____

Thank you for participating in this survey. Your responses will be kept confidential

NOTES: Chapter 7

Date: _____

Things I need to do: _____

Notes:

Chapter 8:
Creating Your Title or Cover Page

A separate title page or cover page enhances the appearance of the proposal and adds to its clarity and makes the proposal more credible. The grant application or RFP will provide guidelines for your cover page. This is a sample of what usually goes on a title page.

The title page consists of the following:

    RFP Announcement number or grant application announcement number

    Title of proposal

    Descriptive subtitle

    Date submitted

    Name and address submitting the proposal

    Telephone number of your organization

    Name of contact person for your organization

    Name of funding organization

    Total amount of request for funding

Below is a sample of a title page for funding. The dates and numbers are fictitious for illustration purposes only. This is only an example. Follow the instruction from the funder if a guide is provided.

Chapter 8: Sample Title Page

Date Submitted to the funder

4/1/2010

RFP #T00.009

Title of Proposal:

Teenage Counseling Program

Subtitle: Proposed Project

Runaway Prevention Program

Name of funding organization you are submitting your proposal to:

The Joy Haven Foundation

Address of funding organization

Address: 333 Sky Blue Avenue

Victory Towne, WI USA

Zip: 30000

SAMPLE TITLE PAGE

Name of your organization: Submitted by the organization

XYZ Organization, Inc.

Address: 111 Hopeville Ave.

Covington, Ca.

Zip: 20080

Contact Person

Bob S. Doess

Telephone number

(516) 444-9999

Total Request Amount

$400,000

Practice worksheet –
Chapter 8 - Create Your Title Page-Fill in the blanks

Date Submitted:
_____

RFP #_____

Title of Proposal:
_____

Subtitle:
_____

Name of funding organization you are submitting your proposal to:
_____

Address of funding organization

Address:_____

_____

Zip:_____

Name of your organization
_____

Address _____

_____

Zip: _____

Contact Person
_____

Telephone #
_____

Total Request Amount

$_____

NOTES: Chapter 8

Date: _____

Things I need to do: _____

Notes:

Chapter 9:
Program Development

Program Activities

1. Describe each activity stated in your proposal. Include every activity proposed. There may be more than one activity.

2. State how the activity will be carried out.

3. What methods will be employed to carry out the activity?

4. Your proposal should have a title – Name the activity program – Methods, project, design and operations

5. Program activities are a description of how your proposal program will be implemented

6. The proposal writer will have an opportunity to demonstrate his or her expertise in program development, training, planning and methodology to the funder.

7. If your proposal has many activities, group the activities together. Example, if you are starting a new program, you will need to locate a facility, form committees such as advisory groups or recruiting staff and training staff. These activities are shown as a subsection under a heading such as preparatory activities.

8. If you have an educational program that will consist of forums, seminars, classes, audio-video movies. These should be grouped under a heading referred to as "Educational Activities."

9. List each program activity in its proper group. Describe each activity under its appropriate heading.

Example:

Planning and preparatory activities

1. Advertise vacant positions
2. Recruit new staff personnel
3. Provide training for new employees
4. Plan for orientation of staff
5. Inform community of new program or project
6. Design brochure for program
7. Select advisory board members
8. Obtain office equipment

Future Plans and Financing for Your Program or Project

Plans for future funding should be addressed in your proposal. This can be explained in the activity section, the letter of intent, in the introduction, or wherever it is asked in the RFP if applicable. If the program is going to generate its own support through fees, contributions, or fundraising activities, it should be indicated to the funding source. If an organization receives initial financial support for one to three years it will become part of a larger ongoing operation. If the organization will receive funding from another source, this funding plan should be described in the proposal. State the exact dollar amount the organization is going to receive from other funding sources for the proposed program. Tell the funder how long the funding will last. State if the funding will support your pilot program or an existing program. When will the funding end? Will the organization be able to write a renewal proposal to continue to support the same program or activity?

Organizational structure: Administration & Staffing

Your organization plan should be discussed in the proposal. The board of directors works closely with administrators of non-profit organizations. The boards of directors are responsible for setting the policies, rules, regulations, practices, and govern the overall operation of a non-profit organization.

The board of directors can strengthen the mission statement of the organization. The organizational plan should include the decision making process, the hierarchy of personnel, lines of communication, and arrangement to assume direction, coordination, and control of the program and project.

Your organization might be linked to another agency. If so, you should describe the relationships between your organization and the partnering agency. State how this other agency supports your organization. What is their contribution? Funders always ask for organizational charts to be submitted in the proposal. Your organization must have an organizational chart to show the funder who is responsible for a certain program or department. Your organization can have more than one chart.

One organizational chart can show the administrative divisions and the other chart shows just the staff of the organization. In nonprofit organizations, an organizational chart shows the entire agency which includes the administrative staff and all of the departments, as well as the staff employed in each position. The same organizational chart also shows the Board of Directors who is ultimately the governing body of the organization.

Officers of the non-profit organization:

The Board of Directors – All of the board members must know the vision, mission, goals and objectives of the organization. The board members are officers of the organization and serve for a specified period of time, on a voluntary basis. They do not receive a salary. Some board of directors can receive reasonable compensation for certain expenditures for reimbursement depending on the non-profit organization policies. Responsibilities of the board members include policy making, fundraising activities for the organization, selection of personnel, establishment of personnel policies, monitoring of all programs and projects. The board handles legal ramifications of the organization. They determine the direction of the organization, vote on specific matters at board of directors meetings. They make recommendations to the organization. Boards for nonprofit organizations can vary in size. Some boards are very small with only three to five members while others are very large. If the organization is large it usually has about seven board members. If an organization is new it is usually very small. However, if an organization has been in existence for many years it can grow to be extremely large. A very large organization can have as many as seven to twenty five board members. The numbers of board members usually consist of an odd number to create a **Quorum** for voting purposes. A Quorum breaks the tie in a vote. The organizations board of directors should be diverse in culture and ethnicity. The board should represent a cross section of the population they are going to serve. The board should have diverse educational backgrounds and experience in specific fields.

Advisory Board – This is an informal group of people that makes recommendations to the organization as it relates to program activities. The advisory board can make recommendations to help enhance or improve programs. They also can help the organization stay focused on the mission of a program or project. They are not usually paid any financial compensation. The role and function of each committee should be described in your proposal if an advisory board is going to be a part of your programs or project to the organization.

STAFFING:

The responsibilities of the **Executive Director** is to develop a good working relationship with the various boards of the organization as well as being familiar with all of the organization's separate committees. The Executive Director attends all Board of Director meetings. He or she sometimes serves as chairman or secretary to the board. The executive director is responsible for overseeing the day to day operations of the entire agency. This person may select and hire staff for the organization. The executive director must approve and sign all proposals before they are sent out to the funding source. If the proposal is not signed it can be rejected by the funder. The signature of the executive director is evidence to the funder that he or she has the authority to submit the organization's proposal for funding of a particular program or project.

Program Directors – Explains the roles, functions, and responsibilities of the staff that will be planning your program activities or projects. This section of your proposal will demonstrate to the funder the administrative managerial ability to assure the funder of an efficiently managed operation.

Staffing Pattern – Staffing your program is done by the Human resource department of the organization. Each staff position should be listed in your proposal with a brief description of responsibilities and qualifications. The amount of time should also be included with each staff position. State if the staff person is employed to work full time, part-time, or a specified number of hours such as 20 hours per week. If the organization is going to use subcontractors such as consultants that are considered experts in a certain field, then the consultant should be mentioned in the proposal.

The organization should submit educational and work experience criteria for each staff person mentioned in the proposal. It doesn't matter if the staff person will be employed full time or part-time you will still need to submit criteria of selection for each position as this will show the funder the qualifications of each person to be employed to work in the proposed program. Salaries do not have to be mentioned at this time. You will have to show each salary in the budget portion of the proposal. The staffing pattern is very important to an organization. It can make a difference between being successful in meeting the mission of the organization as well as the success of the entire proposed program. Don't make the mistake of not budgeting for adequate staffing.

If you are proposing to offer a program that will run 24 hours per day, 7 days per week, and 365 days per year this will require a lot of thought. For example, a "homeless shelter program' where clients actually live in a facility would require 24 hour staff, 7 days per week, 24 hours per day. Make sure your plan covers around the clock personnel to ensure safety and good program control. You will need a lot more staff for a 24 hour operation than if you are running a program or providing services on a daily basis for 8 hours per day, five days per week, Monday thru Friday. For example, if your organization is operating a "child day care program" where small children come only during the day Monday – Friday from 7am – 6pm and closed on Saturday and Sunday, you will need much less staff.

While planning for staffing, give a description of the position. Give the number of staffing required for each position, the responsibilities, and the duration of employment.

Example: One project director full-time 12 months or 52 weeks.

Responsibilities: Overall planning, direction, coordination, management, supervision of the program, liaison with community agencies and organizations, management of fiscal affairs, interpretation of policies and procedures to the community, writing proposals for additional funding for program activities, hire and orientate new staff, conduct evaluation performance reviews of employees, attend meetings, conferences, seminars, represent the agency at community events, write and submit reports to appropriate agency departments as well as write and submit program progress reports to the funding sources.

Example of qualified employees:

Qualifications: A graduate degree in the Human Services field or a Master's of Social Work (MSW), or a Bachelor of Science (BSW) degree in human services with a minimum of 5 years of experience in the field. The applicant must have working knowledge of the program activity that is being proposed in the proposal.

Other program staff may include the following:

1 Executive director, full-time, Master's degree

1 Program coordinator to work full time, Bachelor or Master's degree

1 Contract compliance Manager, Master's degree

1 Quality Assurance Manager, Bachelor or Master's degree

1-3 Accountants –The CFO should be a Certified Public Accountant (CPA)

3 Rehabilitation counselors – full time, Bachelor or Master's degree

4 Social workers, MSW full time, Master's degree

3 Clinical psychologists – full time, PH. D in psychology

2 Medical doctors – part-time/full time, Licensed medical physicians (MD)

2 Nurses – 1 Registered nurse, 1 LPN or LVN(Licensed nurses

1 Teacher- BA or MA degree, Credentials in the field of adult education

1 Human resource director- full-time, Master's degree

Other personnel that may be needed

If you are proposing a program such as a residential care program where participants will live at the facility, you will need staff that can cook meals and clean the facility. Therefore, you may need 1-5 persons to cook meals and 1-5 persons to clean the facility depending on the size of the facility and the number of participants in your proposed program.

In selecting your staff, you want to make sure that each person is highly skilled and qualified to meet the needs of your proposed population. The staff must be able to communicate effectively with the program participants. Make sure the staff is representative of the culture and ethnicity of the people you want to serve. Know your demographics for your proposal. If your proposal is going to assist participants in locating housing, recreational activities, make referrals to other agencies, provide educational training, provide cultural activities, and other services, the organization should add all responsibilities in a job description for each position.

The job specifications or description to each position should be given in an appendix or follow the guidelines in the RFP or grant application.

Additional staffing patterns are as follows:

1 Grant proposal writer full-time

1 Human resource administrative assistant full-time

1 Agency secretary full-time

1 Public relations media person- full-time

1 Attorney – Legal Representation, part-time, on retainer, (law degree)

There are two key positions that are critical to the organization that most non-profit organizations fail or neglect to include in their proposed staffing pattern of their proposal. They are listed as follows:

1. A **Quality Assurance Manager** who is responsible for making sure the organization is developing a set of standards that will assure the funders that the organization is providing a high quality standard program for its participants. The quality assurance manager is responsible for conducting internal audits of the organizations programs or projects. Each activity must be looked at during various intervals to make sure the agency is carrying out the mission statement of the organization or agency. The quality assurance manager makes sure that all programs are implemented on time and are implemented as proposed in the program plan. The quality assurance manager looks for problems within the programs as well as the facility as a whole and is responsible for finding solutions to the problems. The quality assurance manager must know all of the programs that are funded and critique the program's strengths and weaknesses. This person meets with the funders during the evaluation and audit process of the programs funded. The quality assurance manager does damage control for the entire organization. It is the responsibility of the quality assurance manager to be aware of problems that exist within the organization and to come up with solutions to resolve the problems. The quality assurance manager works very closely with the contract compliance manager. As the contract compliance manager works through the requirements for the program being funded, it is the responsibility of the contract compliance manager to bring problems to the quality assurance manager to alert that there is a problem within a particular part of the program. These two positions are imperative to the success of the organization's programs and projects.

2. A **Contract Compliance Manager** is another critical position that some non-profit organizations fail or neglect to include as a part of the staffing pattern. The contract compliance manager is responsible for making sure the organization is in compliance with all awarded contracts from funders. An organization must be compliant with all federal, state, city, or county contracts as well as all other contracts that are in force as a direct result of funding. This is one of the most important

positions to an organization that receives federal, state, city, and county funding. The RFP's are very complex and lengthy. The competition is very stiff. Many other organizations and agencies are applying for the same cycle of funding.

The contract compliance manager is responsible for maintaining and monitoring all of the contracts for the organization once the proposal has been awarded to an agency or organization. Once the organization receives their official letter from the funder notifying them that they have been awarded the funding, the funding agency may require the awarded agency to present other documentation such as insurance policies naming the funder as an additional insured on the organization's insurance policy. The agency will have to show proof that the agency is currently insured with liability insurance to protect the program participants, employees, and others as mandated by the insurance company or the funding agency. The organization can either fax or mail the organization's insurance policy to the funder. The funder will tell the organization what the requirement is for sending the insurance policy. Upon receiving the insurance policy from the organization, a contract for the proposed program or activity will be signed by the funder and the awarded organization. Once both parties have signed the contracts, it is now the responsibility of the contract compliance manager to learn all of the details of the program and make sure the organization is meeting all of the proposal goals and objectives of the funded proposal. This person is responsible for writing and submitting progress reports to the funder and conducting internal audits. The CFO, the program director, and the contract compliance manager all work together on the program progress reports to make sure that all of the information provided to the funder is accurate and complete. The Chief Financial Officer will sign off on all financial reports as it relates to the program's budget.

The contract compliance manager must submit all written reports to the funder in a timely manner. The funder may impose stiff penalties for submitting an audit or a progress report late. If one form is missing from the progress reports, the report is considered to be incomplete by the funder and will be rejected. The funder will notify the contract compliance manager of the missing document(s) and will request that the missing forms be included. Some penalties can range from loss of funding until the funder receives the written report on the programs progress or an agency can lose its funding entirely if the reports are habitually late and the program is proven to be out of contract compliance, the funding agency can stop all future funding. The organization can also risk losing their opportunity to reapply for future funding from their funding sources. If funds are withheld due to reports not being sent to the funder on time, this could negatively impact the organizations ability to continue to deliver the much needed services to its clients. The organization must also answer to their funder, for example the federal government or the state department can ask questions involving reports. There can be other penalties and sanctions including fines imposed on organizations that are found guilty of being out of contract compliance. Program monitoring is essential to any organization that receives funding from any governmental agency such as the City, County, State, or Federal Government funding agencies. Accountability is crucial to receiving tax payer dollars to fund your program or project. There are also legal ramifications for mismanagement of public funds. A word of advice, "when in doubt find out" by seeking legal counsel from your organizations legal representative. Also if a non-profit organization fails to file the required tax documents with the IRS, the organization can run the risk of losing their federal tax exempt status.

The contract compliance manager is responsible for making sure the organization is accountable for all of its activities to the funder per contract agreement. All contracts must be properly executed by both the awarded organization and the funder. The contract will spell out clearly what is expected of the organization. The funder expects the recipient of the grant to adhere to all of the rules & regulations, guidelines, legal aspects, all agreements, budgets, covenants, assurances, certifications, and resolutions. The contract between the funded organization and the funder becomes a legally binding agreement between both parties.

Site Visit -Throughout the funding period, at specified times, a funder will conduct a site visit for the purposes of monitoring for contract compliance. The funder will notify the organization in writing when an auditor will come to the organization's facility to audit its funded program or project. Make sure all of your records are available for inspection.

Sometimes the funder will notify the funded organization of a site visit by telephone. The funder will let the organization know the exact date and time a site visit will be conducted.

Chapter 9: Practice Worksheet:
Program Development-Fill in the blanks

What is your program or project goal? _____
_____
_____
_____

What are the objectives of your program or project? _____
_____
_____
_____
_____

Program or Project Activities: Describe each activity _____
_____
_____
_____
_____

State how your activities will be carried out: _____
_____
_____
_____
_____

What methods will be employed to carry out the activity? _____
_____
_____
_____
_____

How many people serve on your Board of Directors? _____

What is the background of your Board of Directors, i.e. culture/education/experience? Explain
_____
_____
_____
_____
_____

How many people serve on your Advisory Committee? _____

What is the background of the Advisory Committee? Demographics, culture, language, educational? _____
_____
_____
_____
_____

Staffing Pattern: List start up positions. Give titles to each position. How many positions for each title?

Position _____ Education _____

Position _____ Education _____

Position _____ Education _____

Position _____ Education _____

Are there any special qualifications or expertise for each position? Example, credentials
_____
_____
_____
_____
_____

What are the qualifications or expertise for each position? Example, credentials _____
_____
_____
_____
_____

What are the educational requirements? _____
_____
_____
_____
_____

How many full-time positions are needed? _____

How many part-time positions are needed? _____

Will your program or project utilize college interns? Yes _____ No _____
If yes, how many? _____

How will you recruit college intern students? State the method of recruitment. _____
_____
_____
_____
_____

18) Will the student earn college credits for their internship? Explain, Yes _____ No _____
_____
_____
_____
_____

19) At what level will you recruit, Jr. College, University bachelor, master level, or PH.D.
_____
_____
_____
_____

20) Will your program or project solicit volunteers? Yes _____ No _____

If yes, how many volunteers are needed? _____

21). How will you recruit for community volunteers? State the method of recruitment. _____
_____
_____
_____
_____

22). What hours are needed for volunteer services? Time of day? _____

23). Days of the week? _____

24).Who will train your volunteers? _____

NOTES: Chapter 9

Date: _____

Things I need to do: _____

Notes:

Chapter 10:
Capability Statement

The responsibility of convincing a funder that an organization is capable of carrying out a proposed program efficiently and effectively falls upon the organization. The proposal must be presented to the funder in a very well written document. One that is clear in its mission statement, goals, objectives, and strategies. The capability statement should tell the funder how capable the organization is to manage a specific proposed program.

The capability statement should give a brief history of your organization. State the reason why the organization was founded. Give the start date when the organization began. How the organization was initially funded? Where did the funds come from? What was the problem or need that is to be addressed? State the philosophy of the organization. What is the mission statement and goals? State the experience of the organization. Discuss any significant programs that the organization has already developed and implemented. List the organizations achievements. If this is a brand new organization tell what you hope to accomplish in the community. Tell the funder all activities that have been done by the organization and whether the organization has received funding in the past or not. If the organization is proposing a brand new program, it is called a "pilot" program which means the organization has never done this program in the past.

Describe the organizations resources that include the qualifications and background of staff. Who are your board and committee members? How are the board of directors selected? What is the makeup or composition of the board members? Discuss the organizations various committees. Explain resources for offices and equipment. Describe the administrative structure. Describe what mechanisms are in place for financial and programmatic accountability. Be very thorough on how the organization will be accountable to the funding agency. Show evidence of credibility to the funder. State who supports your organization. This could be other non-profit organizations, the business community, community groups, educational institutes, medical facilities, and religious groups. State the size of the organization. Is it small or large? Give the budget amount. Does the organization have a membership in a national organization? Are there any accreditations? Does the organization have endorsements from civic officials and government agencies? Has the organization published any newspaper articles or editorials? State any commendations presented to the organization. Has the organization written publications? Be sure to state how your organization plans to continue the program in the future years to come.

The capability statement can be a section of the proposal or it can be an attachment or appendix. If it is going to be a complete section it should be mentioned in the introduction to the proposal. References to the capability of the organization could be made in the proposed program description or in the introductory section. Make sure your organization can carry out the goals, objectives, and activities of the proposed program. Always remember the mission statement of your organization. Remember why it was established.

Practice worksheet-
Chapter 10: Capability Statement-Fill in the blanks

Give a brief history of your organization

_____
_____
_____
_____
_____
_____

Why was the organization founded? State purpose of the organization:

_____
_____
_____
_____
_____
_____

How was the organization initially funded? _____

_____
_____
_____
_____
_____

State the philosophy of the organization: _____

_____
_____
_____
_____
_____

Chapter 10: Capability Statement

What is the mission statement for the organization? _____
_____
_____
_____
_____
_____

How many years of experience does your organization have in the field for which funds are being sought? _____
_____
_____
_____
_____
_____

List the organizations achievements: _____
_____
_____
_____
_____
_____
_____
_____
_____
_____
_____
_____

What activities have already been done by your organization? List activities: _____
_____
_____
_____
_____
_____

Is this proposed program or project brand new or a pilot? Yes _____ No _____

Describe the organization's resources: i.e. office equipment on hand, _____
_____
_____
_____
_____
_____
_____
_____
_____

Describe your facility. How large is it? How old is the building? What is the square footage? When was the facility built? Give the year. What is the occupancy? _____
_____
_____
_____
_____
_____
_____
_____
_____
_____

How was the facility acquired by the organization? Was the building donated, purchased, or leased? _____
_____
_____
_____
_____
_____
_____
_____
_____
_____

Is the facility currently being leased by the organization? Yes _____ No _____

If yes, how long is the lease contract?_____.

Explain in your own words why you feel your organization is capable of administering the proposed program or project. This is the time to plead your case. Mention your administrative structure as well as your staffing pattern.

_____
_____
_____
_____
_____
_____
_____
_____
_____
_____
_____

Describe the organization's plan for financial accountability: _____
_____
_____
_____
_____
_____

Describe the organization's programmatic accountability: State what mechanism will be in place to monitor your program or project: Who will be responsible for this task?

_____
_____
_____
_____
_____
_____

Who supports your organization? Name the individuals or groups: _____
_____
_____
_____
_____

What is the size of your organization? Small _____ or Large _____. Give total number of employees working for the organization _____.

Does the organization have a membership in a national organization?

Yes _____ No _____ If yes, list the organizations.

_____
_____
_____
_____
_____
_____

Does your organization hold any accreditations? Yes _____ No _____ If yes, what are they? What is the name of the accreditation agency?

_____
_____
_____
_____
_____
_____
_____
_____
_____
_____

13) Does the organization have support from government officials or agencies? Example, Mayor, county commissioners, city council members, school board members, etc.

Yes _____ No _____ If yes, who? What city, what county?

_____
_____
_____
_____

14) Has your organization published any newspaper articles? Yes _____ No _____ If yes, when and where did the article appear? What was the publication date? What was the title of the article or editorial? What was the name of the newspaper? Talk about the article. What was printed about your organization? Was the article positive? _____

_____
_____
_____

15) Has your organization received any special recognition or commendations for work done in the community? Yes _____ No _____. If yes, when was the recognition or commendation given or presented? Give the dates of such recognition and by whom. If the award was given to an individual of the organization what kind of deed warranted the recognition? Anything positive that the organization has done be sure to mention it. This strengthens the proposal.

NOTES: Chapter 10

Date: _____

Things I need to do: _____
_____
_____
_____
_____
_____
_____
_____

Notes:
_____
_____
_____
_____
_____
_____
_____
_____
_____
_____
_____
_____
_____
_____
_____
_____
_____
_____
_____
_____
_____
_____

Chapter 11:
Budget Component

The budget should relate to the goals and objectives of your proposal. The budget consists of a specific dollar that is requested in a proposal. Most governmental agencies will provide their own forms to be completed and submitted with the proposal. Foundations do not provide the same forms to fill out as government agencies.

The funding agency wants to make sure that your proposed budget for your organization is realistic and that all of the money that is being solicited is truly needed. The funding agency must be convinced that the organization requesting the funding can demonstrate managerial and administrative skills. The funder also needs to feel the organization has the capability of handling the budget.

The budget forms provided by government agencies should be clearly and neatly filled out by an experienced accountant preferably by a Certified Public Accountant (CPA) or an accountant that has many years of experience submitting budgets to a government agency. The government will stress guidelines in their Request for Proposal (RFP) related to the budget. Read the (RFP) carefully. It will tell the grant writer and the Chief Financial Officer (CFO) what is an allowable or non-allowable expense.

A government (RFP) will state the amount of available funding through a Notice of Funds Availability (NOFA). The exact dollar amount will tell the proposal writer how much money is available to apply for. A word of CAUTION, DO NOT request more money than is offered in the RFP announcement. If your budget is greater than the available amount you have already cancelled your organization from being awarded the grant. Funders will not exceed their own budgets. Keep your budget in the range that is announced in the RFP. You can use realistic estimates to calculate your budget. Do your homework by contacting local employment agencies to find out the going rates for a particular job position for employment purposes. Do a comparable or comparison with other agencies surrounding your proposed area of services to find out what the salaries are for positions you want funding for. If you want a quality program you will have to employ professional staff that will provide the best possible services. The staff may be required to hold special credentials or advanced degrees to carry out the goals and objectives of your proposed program. The staff will demand respectful salaries for their experience, education, and expertise. This usually requires higher salaries to attract high quality staff. In order to compete for quality staff, they must also be offered a solid fringe benefit package that includes medical, dental, and vision insurance along with other company benefits. The proposal writer must submit a budget that will pay for all of the program needs.

Some proposal writers will include excessive expenses in a budget. This is called "Padding". The funders can recognize this. This is not recommended. Also, some proposal writers will include the term "miscellaneous" to their line item budget. This is not an acceptable practice. Miscellaneous means anything can be added to the budget at anytime. Most funders will not allow miscellaneous expenses. They want to know up front exactly what they are paying for. The budget must have a clear dollar amount for a proposed program or project.

As a proposal writer, do not make the mistake of reducing the budget to an unrealistic amount where it is impossible to carry out the program activities adequately or effectively. Some organizations think it is better to reduce the budget and hope the funder will give them something towards the program rather than nothing. This kind of thinking is a mistake. Reducing the dollars in the budget will create problems in the program later on. Funders are also experienced in knowing how much a program or project will cost. If your budget is too low that may work against you.

The personnel budget must include all of the positions described in the staffing pattern of the proposal. Do not add staff later if it was not previously mentioned. The budget should not show a salary for a position that is not previously discussed. The budget should provide sufficient funds to implement all activities listed in the program activity section of the proposal. Budget explanation notes should be on a separate sheet. In preparing the budget, do not add expenditures to cover items that were not mentioned in the narrative material. For example, if you did not mention your organization was going to create and publish a monthly newsletter to be distributed to interested individuals or distribute in the community or join a professional group where there are dues annually, you can't later add a budget line item for these expenditures. Only activities mentioned previously in the proposal can be funded.

Another important part of the budget is the in-kind contributions or donated items. You must show this financial support in your proposed budget. While some in-kind contributions may not be monetary, if your organization had to pay for the in-kind contribution, it still has a dollar value. Some funders will ask if you will have any in-kind contributions to support your program or project. This may be listed on a separate sheet or could be listed directly with the budget page. Follow the instructions in the RFP. If any questions arise regarding the RFP, ask the funder for clarification. Follow the rules and procedures of the funding agency. Funders are more responsive to proposals when you meet all of their requirements.

All proposals consist of a budget. This is the major component to the proposal. Once the funder reads through your proposal and sees all the wonderful things your organization wants to accomplish, the question is raised, "how much" is this going to cost? Therefore, the budget must be realistic, logical, and sound.

Budgets consist of expenses or costs, income, and in-kind contributions, expenses and costs are shown in dollar amounts. In-kind contributions are items donated by individuals, groups, corporations, businesses, and volunteer services.

Individuals that volunteer their time and lend their skills, talents, expertise, and their willingness to help others adds an invaluable asset to your organization. Volunteers provide thousands of hours to organizations which helps keep down the cost of expenses in a non-profit budget. Enough cannot be said about how much money volunteers save non-profit organizations annually. If your organization is going to utilize volunteers, be sure to mention this in your proposal. Volunteers usually provide services to non-profit organizations on a part-time basis. These are individuals that may be retired, college students, or people who are employed by corporations who want to give back to the community or society. These individuals want to give of their time. Volunteers usually volunteer at agencies or organizations where their own personal interest is a match with the mission statement of an organization. Rarely do volunteers provide free services on a full-time basis. Even large corporations will send their employees to non-profit organizations such as schools to work with children. Some employees are encouraged to participate in major fundraisers for a worthy cause for example a United Way campaign. This is a corporation's way of giving back to society.

The budget should be done only by the organizations Chief Financial Officer (CFO) and other accounting staff selected by the organization. The organization might even contract with an outside accounting firm to assist in the financial dealings of the organization. This position preferably should be filled by a person who is a CPA as this person will be responsible for administering and overseeing all of the funding that comes to the organization. This person should be well versed in the tax structure, salaries and wages, personnel fringe benefits packages, subcontractors, consultants, expenditures for equipment and supplies to run the program or project. When a program is audited for program progress and accountability, the CFO is the first person the funder wants to meet with. The Chief Financial Officer (CFO) is the key person that is held responsible for the accountability of the expenses of a funded program.

Funders do not like "sloppy accounting practices". Funders do not want their money co-mingled with other funding sources. Once a funder has awarded an organization funds for a specific program or project, the CFO must establish a separate account to identify that particular fund. Each proposal funded has a legal contract number. The contract number is assigned by the funding source. If the funding source is a governmental agency such as federal, city, state, or county, once the contract is executed all correspondence will be referenced by the contract number of the grant award. The contract number is like an identification number.

Both the funder and the organization will identify the program by the <u>contract number</u>. A word of caution, <u>do not mix money with other funding monies</u>. If co-mingling of funds occurs, your organization will be immediately out of <u>contract compliance</u>. All funding from all sources must be kept separate. Even if another funder provides additional money to the same program or project, this money still must be kept separate and have its own account number to which the money is applied. As the program uses the money, the funds are drawn against its own account.

Co-mingling of funds can put your organization's program in trouble. You can run out of money due to mismanagement of funds. The money must be spent on the specific program which was stated in your proposal. Co-mingling of funds means money that was supposed to fund your program was used to support another program. This is an unprofessional accounting practice. If the funder learns that your organization is mixing or co-mingling their money with other funding sources this would make the funder very unhappy. It would be very difficult for the funder to audit the books for your proposed program. This creates a big problem for the funder. An organization is sending a message to the funder that they are not capable of money management. An organization must be able to demonstrate to a funder that they can handle budgets of any size.

A non-profit organization should have a separate accounting department that is staffed with full-time accountants that are qualified to develop budgets for proposals. All of the accountants do not need to be a CPA, but should have an advanced degree in business and accounting such as an MBA. Some responsibilities may require someone with a bachelor's degree. It is up to the organization on how they want to manage and oversee their budgets. The accounting department can have staff that may a Bachelors degree with an accounting background and a lot of experience working in the field of accounting. The accountants should function with a very high degree of professionalism and integrity. Honesty should be a virtue of an accountant of a nonprofit organization. An organization can lose its funding if an accountant is found to be incapable of managing the business affairs of the organization. Accountability in terms of the program operation and its fiscal management is critical to developing a professional reputation with funders.

Penalties can be imposed on organizations who mismanage their funds. The organization also runs the risk of negative publicity that will ultimately ruin the integrity of the organization. Negative publicity has a profound impact on future funding to the organization. The organization should have a check and balance system in the accounting department. All work should be checked by other accountants. If anything looks irregular or if a discrepancy occurs, it needs to be addressed immediately and the problem corrected as soon as the discrepancy is found. This is not the time to turn the other way and pretend the problem does not exist. Nor is it the time to point the fingers of blame. Just correct the problem and move on. Do not under any circumstance attempt to cover up corruption in the accounting department. This kind of practice will come back to haunt the organization and can hurt its reputation and damage its integrity. Keep your accounting books in a position in where the numbers can withstand extreme scrutiny if necessary by any funder.

The CFO is responsible for providing funders with ongoing financial reports for each program or project as mandated by the funder or funding agency. Governmental agencies require different reporting mechanisms than foundations or private donors. Governmental agencies will let you know what their reporting rules and procedures are. They have reporting cycles. Governmental agencies will let your organization know far in advance when all reports are due. Some funders require monthly progress reports or quarterly reports. The executed contract that was signed by both the funding agency and the awarded organization will state the reporting requirements. Make sure all reports are submitted to the funding agency on or before the due date to avoid any late filing penalties. Programs or projects must be developed and implemented as promised in your proposal utilizing the funding that is awarded to your organization. The accountant will keep the proper books, and ledgers for all expenditures connected to the funded program or project.

Budget expenses include personnel staff, salaries and wages, fringe benefits, consultants, direct expenses, and indirect expenses. Most governmental agencies will provide a section in the RFP which has its own forms of how to complete the budget section of your organizations proposal. Foundation or other private donors will have different guidelines and requirements for submitting a budget for funding. A foundation may support only a small portion of a program that may already be in existence or a new program. Their budget may not be as extensive as a government document.

Expense Budget

Personnel

1. Salaries and wages paid to part-time and full time staff considered regular employees

2. Fringe benefits or employee benefits

3. Consultants, subcontractors, non-regular employees

Find out the pay scale for similar jobs within other organizations or local public or private employment agencies. Salaries should be in a range that will attract highly qualified professional individuals. If the program is going to support a 12 month position, it should be reflected in the budget showing the salary for 1 year. However, if the position is not filled because the position is brand new and the employee may start working 2 months into the implementation of the program, the budget may be reduced to show a ten month operation of the program instead of 12 months. The annual salary rate must be shown, but only 10 months of actual salary should be included in the expenditure amount column. The budget should reflect whether this is a full time or part-time position, and for how many months the position will be held, and an accurate salary for the position.

Contractors, Subcontractors, Consultants

Contractors, subcontractors, or consultants are not considered employees of the organization. They are hired on a per diem or unit cost basis. Some nonprofit agencies will pay subcontractors all monies due once an invoice is submitted by the subcontractor to the organization for services rendered. The subcontractor is regarded as a 1099 under the government tax reporting code. Nonprofit organizations may not take any taxes out of the subcontractors pay. The contractors are responsible for filing their own taxes. Subcontractors or contractors are not entitled to fringe benefits as regular employees of the organization. They are self employed and are responsible for reporting their earnings as required by law.

The subcontractor or contractor will enter into a written contract agreement which will state the scope of work or services to be performed and provided for a non-profit organization. The contract will also state the duration of the project. It specifies how long it will take to start and complete a specific task. The contract agreement will state all financial agreements and how the contractor is to be paid for services rendered. Once the contractor and the organizations authorized representative executes the contract by signing it, the contract now becomes a legally binding document. The contractors and subcontractors are aware that they are not entitled to fringe benefits offered to regular employees of the organization.

Fringe Benefits

Fringe benefits are expenses for social security, retirement plans, health insurance, dental, vision, group life insurance, worker's compensation, unemployment compensation, state disability insurance, and other costs deemed by the organization.

A sample budget has been included. The figures are used for illustration purposes only. The numbers are fictitious and do not represent current rates. Check with your insurance carriers in your local area. Check also with your government agencies for specific rates.

Sample Budget

Social Security	8.0%
State Unemployment	4.0%
State Disability	3.0%
Worker's Compensation	5.0%
Employee Retirement Plan	3.0%
Group Health	2.0%
Group Life Insurance	0.4%
Disability Insurance	0.6%
Dental Insurance	0.6%
Vision Insurance	0.4%
Total	**27%**

Consultants

State in your proposal each type of consultant, the rate of pay, scope of work, number of work days, and number of hours to perform a specific task for the organization. The consultant should be stated in your proposal narrative. Describe what the consultant will do in the staffing section of the proposal. Do not add the consultant in the budget if the consultant was not mentioned in the proposal. The proposal should justify the need for the consultant. Some government agencies have specific policies and guidelines for the use of consultants and the rate of reimbursement. The consultant is usually compensated on a per diem basis.

The consultant's scope of work must be clear and concise. Governmental agencies will approve consultants to perform specific tasks for nonprofit organizations for a specified period of time. You may ask the funding agency staff for its written regulations regarding the use of consultants and contract services. Government agencies have established rates for how much they are willing to pay for a consultant to provide technical assistance to a non-profit organization. The government will compensate an approved consultant on a reimbursement basis for traveling expenses, lodging, and 3 meals per day. The consultant pays for all expenses up front out of pocket and then submits an invoice to the government funding agency for reimbursement. The consultant is responsible for submitting all receipts for reimbursement expenses. The government funding agency will provide a consultant package giving all of the details of how consultants should submit invoices for reimbursement. Be sure to follow all of the guidelines, rules, and regulations regarding consulting compensation given to you by the funding agency or organization.

Other Direct Expenses
Travel Expenses

Travel by staff, consultants, board members, and if necessary program participants must be justified. State the reason for the travel. Is the travel trip necessary? The detail and justification for travel costs should be shown in the budget itself or in a budget explanation note. Out of town or long distance travel must be shown separate from local travel mileage. Car rentals and air travel must appear as separate items under "Travel Expenses". Some funders will allow payment for mileage, meals, and lodging to attend meeting, conferences, or seminars. The organization must request this in the budget. A travel log must be maintained for reimbursement for mileage.

Per diem - This represents the reimbursement to individuals for hotel and meals. The budget should show the number of days to be reimbursed and the amount to be paid per day.

Office Supplies - (Consumables) Consist of stationary, business cards, pens, pencils, and paper,

Program Supplies - Training materials, instructional materials, and similar items to be purchased.

Equipment - Desks, copy machines, fax machines, computers, printers, telephones, etc. Each item and its purchase or rental cost should be listed and the total shown in the expenditures column. Funders will let you know in writing what equipment they will fund and what they won't fund. You may need to contact the funder while you are writing the proposal to find out exactly what the funder will allow in the budget. Refer also to the "RFP" to see if the funder has mentioned what type of equipment is allowable for funding.

Telephone - Show monthly estimate for telephone bill. Include number of telephones.

Rent - Show cost of office space rental indicating cost per square foot. Indicate number of square feet. How much will it cost to rent per year? Give dollar amount. Example: $1.00 per square foot. State if there is remodeling or renovation involved. This is an annual expenditure.

Other Expenditures Items - These items should be listed individually. These items are postage, printing of reports, agency memberships in other organizations, special insurance, purchase of publications, and utilities if not included in the rent. Conferences should also be included in the budget.

Here is an example of an equipment budget. These numbers are used only for the purpose of illustration and do not represent today's cost.

3 chairs @ $100.00 each =	$300.00
3 desk @ $125.00 each =	$375.00
1 typewriter @ $200.00 =	$200.00
1 computer @ $1000.00 =	$1000.00
1 printer @$500.00 =	$500.00
1 file cabinet @$200.00 =	$200.00
2 telephones @$50.00 =	$100.00
Total	**$2,675.00**

Do not include a miscellaneous item. Funders do not like miscellaneous items. The budget should show specific items of expenses. Your budget should show the funder that careful planning went into developing the budget estimates.

Indirect Cost

Indirect expense is called overhead. Overhead costs are costs shared by all on organization's activities and programs, such as the cost of the audit, the executive director's salary, and general liability insurance. Indirect costs are the ones that are essential to all agency programs, but difficult to assign in specific amounts to any one program.

Due to the fact that special projects and programs benefit from agency functions classified as overhead costs, it is important to include a portion of these costs in the requests for funding. Government agencies sets a maximum allowable percentage for indirect costs. After you have estimated your total direct expenses, you may be able to add a line item such as indirect costs at a percentage allowable by the funding agency.

You cannot list the same equipment on a line item as direct cost and indirect cost. It has to be one or the other. For example, if you included a copy machine as a part of your organization's overhead or indirect costs, you cannot include the copies as a direct expense. You will need to contact foundations to find out what their maximum indirect cost rate is. Foundations don't want to pay more than the organization's fair share of the proposal program.

Matching Grant

A matching grant is when a funder donates a percentage of the budget and the organization matches the donation dollar for dollar. Matching funds are a type of leverage grant.

In-kind Contributions

In-kind contributions are a donation to a project or program in the form of goods and services where there is no cash involved. Volunteer services and clothing donations are examples of in-kind contributions.

Functional or Program Budgets

A funder may request a functional or program budget in addition to the line by line budget. A program or functional budget requires that the total expenditures be allocated to the major functions or program components. This is money allotted to each category.

Identify the major functional activities or program categories such as administration, intake, health education, community relations, counseling services, training education, information and referral. In complex programs, a major program category can be further divided into subcategories. For example, counseling could be broken down into counseling youth, counseling adults, and counseling aging persons.

Prepare a budget that shows all of the categories and the total dollar cost for each category. Attach a sheet describing how the total for each category was reached. Example for allocated functional budget, a program manager at $50,000 a year might devote 1/2 time on administration 1/4 time on community relations, 1/4 time on health education.

Example of allocation of function or program budget:

$30,000 to administration

$10,000 to community relations

$10,000 to health education

Giving a total of $50,000 for this full-time position

A word of advice, make sure the accountant checks and double checks the numbers in the budget. If the numbers are incorrect, the proposal may not be selected for funding. Make sure that the total amount requested in the proposal does not exceed the amount that the funder is announcing for funding. Make sure the budget is presented in the format requested by the funder.

Under Utilized Funding

An organization is awarded funding for a particular program, but all of the money was not used as proposed. For example, a counseling center is awarded monies to counsel high risk teens for one year, but all of the money was not used. What happens to the extra money left over from the grant? As your program is in operation, the progress should be monitored to make sure you are reaching the number of people you said that you were going to serve. You are now in the tenth month of your program with only two months left to use all of the funds for your program. You find out that you have $30,000 that must be used before the grant period is up, but you know that you will not be able to spend the money during the next two months. What should you do? The executive director or the organization's CFO should contact the funding agency and let the funder know that the organization will have a reserve of $30,000 at the end of the grant period. The funder can remedy the situation in a couple of ways. (1) They can ask that the funding be returned or (2) they can approve the organization to submit what is called a grant modification proposal. This allows the organization to expand the program and allow more participants to benefit from the program initially proposed. In this case, the organization gets to keep all of the money. No money is returned to the funder.

When an organization starts a brand new pilot program, it is hard to determine if all of the funds are going to be used. Sometimes participants for whom the program was designed to serve, do not take advantage of the programs and services which is being offered to them or their community. This is one reason why funds sometimes are underutilized. Rarely will the funder ask for the money to be returned. It is recommended that the organization use all of the money that is awarded to them. If the organization doesn't use all of the funds, the funder may remember this when the organization reapplies for funding. The organization runs the risk of getting their budget reduced to prevent another over payment situation.

It is very important that the organization do all that they can to market and promote new start up programs to ensure that the entire community as well as other service oriented non-profit organizations are aware of any newly funded program so that the individuals the program was designed to serve does in fact get to benefit from this funding.

The program your organization is proposing may be funded by many different sources. Your program can be funded by governmental agencies, foundations, and corporate sponsorship. Many funders are more comfortable when a program is funded by other funding partners. Other income may come from special events, fees for services, or individual contributions. Each source of revenue support should be mentioned in the budget. These can be estimated numbers.

Funders want to see a balanced budget. Funders do not want to support programs that will end the funding period with either a large deficit or a major surplus of cash. In-kind donations should be shown in your budget as revenue and expense.

Example of a Sample Budget

	Cash Required	In-Kind Contributions	Total Budget
Expected Revenue			
Grants			
Foundations	$150,000		$150,000
Government	$100,000		$100,000
Corporations	$35,000		$35,000
Individual Contributions	$75,000		$75,000
Special events (net)	$50,000	$40,000	$50,000
In-kind donations			
Total Revenue	$410,000	$40,000	$410,000
Expected Expenses			
Salaries			
Program Coordinator	$50,000		$50,000
Social Worker I	$45,000		$45,000
Social Worker II	$48,000		$48,000
Administrative Assistant	$35,000		$35,000
Executive Director (part-time: $70,000 x 20%)	$14,000		$14,000
Benefits (20% of salaries)	$40,000		$40,000
Contract personnel	$45,000	$10,000	$55,000
Program services		$15,000	$15,000
Total personnel	$277,000	$25,000	$302,000
Office rent	$15,000		$15,000
Insurance	$6,000		$6,000
Printing	$15,000	$5,000	$20,000
Equipment	$30,000	$10,000	$40,000
Office Supplies	$8,000		$8,000
Utilities	$5,000		$5,000
Telephone	$4,000		$4,000
Copy Services	$10,000		$10,000
Postage	$11,000		$11,000
Travel	$8,000		$8,000
Membership dues	$800		$800
Total non personnel	$112,800	$15,000	$127,800
Total expenses	$389,800	$40,000	$429,800

NOTES: Chapter 11

Date: _____

Things I need to do: _____

Notes:

Chapter 12:
Budget Audits

This grant writing guide is focusing on funding for non-profit organizations that receive or want to receive funding from governmental agencies such as the federal government, state government, city government, and county governments. All non-profit organizations across this nation are entitled to apply for funding for projects and programs from governmental agencies. These are tax payer dollars. Please use the funds wisely if your project or program is funded.

Due to the fact that all government monies are usually collected from tax payers, these funding agencies have strict guidelines when they fund nonprofit organizations. All government agencies conduct periodic internal audits of all of the non-profit organizations that they fund. The governmental agencies gives every non-profit organization a set of rules, procedures, and guidelines about how the funds should be spent. The organization must understand the rules of contract compliance and stay within the confines of the program or project budget.

It is very important that the executive director of non-profit organizations work very closely with the Chief Financial Officer to monitor the expenditures of any federal, state, city, or county funding as well as private donations. If during an audit, the governmental funding source finds any deficiencies, the organization is given a written document citing any and all deficiencies. The organization is given a certain amount of time to correct the deficiency. If the deficiency or deficiencies are not corrected the funder can legally withhold any additional money until the organization fixes or resolves the problems that were cited in the audit.

The organization's programs are audited as well as the budget. There are penalties for not correcting deficiencies. If there is evidence of gross mismanagement, the government agencies can impose different types of penalties for inappropriate use of funds. Any accountant working with government funds must realize the severe penalties that can be imposed on a non-profit organization for misuse of funds. The funding agency can tell the organization what kinds of penalties or consequences can be imposed for misuse of funds. There is usually written literature on this issue.

The non-profit organization staff cannot use tax payer dollars for their personal use outside of their regular legal salary. It is recommended that non-profit organizations use an outside accounting firm to conduct internal audits and have annual financial reports done for in house use. Some funders will even ask for audit and annual reports when an organization is submitting a proposal for funding. Funders that are not connected to the government will also conduct internal budget audits. Don't move money from one line item to another without written permission from a funder, or the federal, state, city, or county governments. All funders want to believe that they have contributed to a reputable organization and that the organization will use the funds for its intended purposes per contract agreement.

Any funder can ask for part or all of the money funded to an organization be returned if they discover that the funds are being abused or mismanaged. The funder will give organizations ample time to correct all deficiencies whether programmatic or budget. The executive director, the board of directors, and chief financial officer (CFO) are held accountable for all expenditures and how programs and services are provided. If audits are showing problems, the organization is obligated to come up with a corrective action plan to resolve the problem.

If your organization has received a grant from any governmental agency you will be audited for the accountability of the use of funds. When you receive a brand new grant, you cannot use money awarded from the new grant to pay bills that were incurred prior to the new grant monies. You can't rob Peter to pay Paul. All funding accounts must be kept separate. If you co-mingle funds, the organization will have a difficult time explaining this practice to a government auditor or a private donor. Be prepared to answer questions from the auditor. Auditors expect you to be in contract compliance. They expect the organization to be honest in handling all monies awarded to the organization.

Remember the people you are serving are depending on your organization to help meet their needs. An organization may not be able to continue to offer services if they lose their funding due to mismanagement of funds. The organization is at risk of losing funding from other funding sources if there is evidence of financial mismanagement. The reputation of the organization will now be viewed in a negative way. Mismanagement of funds and not filing required reports or financial records to the IRS can lead to putting the organizations 501(c)(3) tax exempt status in jeopardy of losing its tax exempt status. Accounting records are very important for maintaining the tax exempt recognition. A tax document 990N is usually required of most nonprofit organizations except churches. Check with the Internal Revenue Service (IRS) USA.

The organization should avoid any kind of negative publicity. The grant writer wants to stress positive information to the funder. Stay away from negative comments. The negative publicity can hit the news media quickly which will certainly impact the integrity of the organization.

Any funder that provides money to any non-profit organization can audit an organization's books at any time. If you accept their money, they have a legal right to monitor how your organization is managing their money. Don't risk losing your funding. Make sure your organization has a chief financial officer (CFO) who is a certified accountant on staff that functions with a high degree of honesty and credibility. Your organization should have an impeccable reputation built on integrity.

NOTES: Chapter 12

Date: _____

Things I need to do: _____
_____
_____
_____
_____
_____
_____
_____

Notes:
_____
_____
_____
_____
_____
_____
_____
_____
_____
_____
_____
_____
_____
_____
_____
_____
_____
_____
_____
_____
_____
_____
_____

Chapter 13:
Developing a Grant Writing Team

For non-profit organizations, a successful grant requires a team effort which means that the organization must select key staff in the organization that have extensive knowledge and expertise in the area of writing grant proposals. The writers must have the ability to be creative in their thought process. Good grant writers develop their own unique approaches as to how they want to convey their ideas for presentation of a grant proposal. Since writing a proposal is usually done as a team effort, all individuals involved must appreciate each person's individuality and have confidence in the other team member's ability and experience.

Each person will have their own methods as to how to present a proposal to a funder. The most important aspect to writing as a team is to show respect for each team member's ability and skills. The ultimate goal is to present to the funder a clear and concise presentation of the problem which needs to be addressed. Writing proposals can be a lot of work, yet very rewarding. This is a field where an artistic person or a creative person can truly utilize their intellect. Writing proposals is truly a skill. The proposal grant writer must have good writing skills and be able to communicate effectively in written communication as well as verbal communication.

In selecting people to write a grant proposal for your organization, you must identify individuals who enjoy writing grant proposals. The process can be very long and tedious or short and easy. It depends on the funder and the RFP requirements or the grant application and the length of time the grant writer has to prepare the proposal. It takes many hours to devote to writing a grant. If the agency or organization is very large and is asking for millions of dollars to fund several programs in the same RFP proposal it can take at least six people to write a grant proposal as a team. The grant writing process is too tedious for just one person to do alone if the grant is requesting millions of dollars. If your organization is asking for a large sum of money, which government agencies do award in the six figures or millions of dollars for one RFP announcement, it is necessary to have a good writing team in place.

It is not impossible for one person to write a grant proposal if the requested grant amount is very small. For example, if a grant is under $10,000 dollars, one person can write the grant proposal with the assistance of an accountant and a secretary. If the grant writer is competent in math and feels comfortable with writing the budget, and is a good typist, this person could handle the entire proposal alone. However, this is not recommended. Even a small grant needs staff support. The chief financial officer or an accountant still needs to do the budget portion for accuracy even on a small grant.

Grant proposals should not be written in a vacuum. No one should feel like the lone ranger in putting a grant proposal together for funding. For a large organization that is seeking millions of dollars in funding, a grant team should consist of a researcher, accountant, department heads, department managers, program coordinators, secretary, and typist. A person will be needed for gathering data such as reports, support letters, Memorandum of Understanding (MOU's), and Memorandum of Agreement (MOA's), certifications, assurances, insurance policies, and all necessary attachments as required by the funder.

It is the responsibility of the executive director, board of directors, or a department head to identify funding for the organization. The executive director or other appropriate staff of the organization determines if an RFP announcement fits the organization's mission statement or if the RFP meets other goals and objectives of the organization. The executive director or the appropriate appointed staff will submit a letter of intent to the funder if the organization wants to apply for the funding.

The grant writing team will immediately begin to work on the proposal once the letter of intent is mailed to the funder. The first meeting of the grant writing team is usually presided by the department head that is going to receive the funding. The team is informed of the RFP and its requirement. A brainstorming meeting is usually held with the team to discuss which approach or method they will use to accomplish the task of writing the grant proposal. A leader of the grant writing team is selected at this first meeting. The leader of the team must demonstrate excellent leadership skills. The leader must be well organized and focused on the task at hand. Above all, the leader must be a good listener and a good team player. The team leader must be able to take suggestions and recommendations from other team members and be willing to have open discussions concerning new ideas to write the best possible grant proposal. The leader must be able to command respect from the rest of the team. Leadership skills are essential in grant writing because it is the leader of the team who is responsible for guiding the grant writing process. The leader of the grant writing team should have experience in grant writing to be able to give direction to the other team members. The leader of the grant writing team may not be the department head. Rather it might be a manager of the department who is going to receive the funding. The department head is still responsible for monitoring the progress and process of the grant proposal.

The grant writing team should be relieved of other organizational obligations or tasks so that they can focus only on getting the proposal written. Some RFP's do not give a lot of time for writing proposals. Sometimes there may be only 1-2 months to accomplish this project. This can be a very stressful time for the grant writing team, especially if they are pressed for time. This is a time all of the departments in the organization who will be affected by this project should give their full cooperation to the grant writing team. For example, if the RFP's requires a biography and qualifications of personnel who will work on the project or program to be submitted with the proposal, then it is the responsibility of the Human Resource department of the organization to give this information to the person on the grant writing team who is responsible for gathering this information. If the biographies are not submitted as requested in the grant proposal application, the organization would risk being denied the funding it is seeking.

While the proposal is being written, it should be reviewed and evaluated at intervals throughout the process. By doing this, the team will catch errors before the entire proposal is finished. The reviewers of the proposal can suggest corrections as the proposal is being developed. After the proposal is written, at least three people in the organization should review the proposal for accuracy and content. Make sure all certifications, insurance documents, attachments, letters of support, assurances, and all other required documents are included.

The proposal is usually written in three drafts. The proposal is proof read and edited after which a final proposal is written and prepared in its final stage to be presented to the funder. The final proposal should be reviewed by at least three people for accuracy and to make sure all corrections are made prior to submitting the proposal to the funder. The proposal needs to be looked at very critically using the RFP checklist as a guide for all requirements to insure that every question has been answered as clearly as possible.

The three people who should review the final proposal are:

1. The executive director

2. The organization's chief financial officer (CFO) a CPA accountant

3. The director or department head or anyone who has experience in writing grant proposals. It can also be reviewed again for the very last time by someone on the grant writing team.

The executive director needs to review the proposal because the final product will have to be signed by this person before it is sent to the funder. The chief financial officer has to review the proposal because this person will be responsible for all expenditures if the project is funded. The chief financial officer (CFO) will provide the numbers in the budget for the proposed project or program. The department head of the department that will benefit from the funds should also review the final draft. For example, if the grant funding is for a youth program, the person that is the department head for the youth services division should review the final proposal. All three reviewers will read the entire proposal and make any corrections. Once all of the corrections are made and the final proposal is written, the executive director can now sign the original proposal which includes all of the legal required documents. Once the original proposal is signed, copies of the proposal will be made. The RFP or grant application will give guidelines as to how many copies of the proposal are needed to be sent to the funder.

The original proposal should be signed first by the executive director before copies are made. Sometimes the signatures are needed by the board members or the Chairperson of the board of directors. This stipulation will be stated in the RFP application. All signatures should be authentic and signed in black or blue ink. Do not use red or purple ink. These colors do not show well on copies. The signature should not be an electronic signature or a rubber stamp. Using electronic signatures and rubber stamps are unacceptable signatures. This is unacceptable to the funder. All attachments should also have original signatures. The original proposal must contain all hand written signatures.

Now the proposal is ready to be sent to the funder. Some "request for proposals" (RFP) requires a resolution document that is voted on by the organization's board of directors. This resolution authorizes the organization to apply for the funding. Each board member votes on the resolution and their signature represents their attendance at the board meeting in which the executive director was given the approval to apply for the funding. Each board member must sign the resolution document. The board members cannot use electronic signatures or rubber stamps. The resolution is included with the proposal when submitted to the funder. The process of submitting your proposal to the funder is discussed in Chapter 16.

Practice worksheet-Grant Writing Development Team

Select Individuals that will be responsible for writing the grant proposal. Assign one task to each team person. Include the individual's area of experience and knowledge. You may have as many people as the organizations needs on the grant writing team. However, you don't want too many. A team of three to six people is usually sufficient. If it is a small grant it may require only one to 3 people. Example of a small grant might be an RFP for $10,000 dollars or less. If it is a very large grant it may require five to six people. Example of a large grant might be $10 million or more. This size grant may require a team of five or six team members. The larger the grant amount requested, you may need more people to write the grant application or grant proposal.

Name of program or project: _____

Department submitting the proposal for funding: _____

Example

Individual's Name	Responsibility/Task
1. John D. K. (example)	Certified public accountant (CPA) Head of finance department 5 years of experience
2.	
3.	
4.	
5.	
6.	
7.	

NOTES: Chapter 13

Date: _____

Things I need to do: _____
_____
_____
_____
_____
_____
_____

Notes:
_____
_____
_____
_____
_____
_____
_____
_____
_____
_____
_____
_____
_____
_____
_____
_____
_____
_____
_____
_____

Chapter 14:
Sustainability Component

How will your organization continue its program once the initial funding has ceased or run out? This is an area that needs to be looked at seriously while writing the proposal for initial funding. Often times the funders would like to know how the organization will sustain the program once the funding has ended.

The organization will have to continue to look for funding from other sources to keep the program going even if the initial funder no longer provides funds for a particular program. When a program is terminated due to inadequate continuation funding, it often fails to meet its goal. The organization will have to plan fundraising activities that will aid in expanding programs already in existence or to support new programs or projects.

In a capital or equipment proposal, which includes purchasing major equipment or building renovations and expansions, the funder will need to know the costs your organization will incur in operating the new equipment, maintaining a new building, or increasing services, and what your organization has for meeting these costs.

Future funding can come from the following sources:

1. Foundation and corporations that support on-going programs.

2. Annual Campaigns which derives donations from membership drives.

3. Fundraising Activities- Hold special events that generates large amounts of money for the organization.

4. Fees for Services- Charging a fee for services can offset the budget. If the organization is going to charge fees to clients or program participants this needs to be addressed in the proposal. The organization needs to determine the fee scale

on how much to charge each client or participant and then determine how much in additional donations are needed to meet the revenue target.

5. Solicitation for donations- Nonprofit organizations can solicit donations from the private sector such as businesses.

6. Sales of items- Your organization may be able to set up a gift shop, a small restaurant, or thrift store, and run a profitable sales program to increase revenue for your program.

7. Activities- The organization could hold a musical concert, sell books, sell music CD's, DVD's, plan social events, or plan trips, etc. The money raised from these sales might help cover some of the program cost. A clear expense and revenue projection should be part of your proposal.

Funders do not always know how the organization is going to continue future funding. However, it is a good idea to include some information on sources of money for the program's future.

If the funder does want an explanation as to how the organization is going to continue the program once funding has ended, be specific with the funder explaining how the program will continue once the funding has ended. Reassure the funder your commitment that your organization will seek other funding resources before their funding has ended. Show the funder the effort your organization is making to make sure the program they have funded will continue. Discuss your organizations strategies to keep funding coming in on a continuous basis.

NOTES: Chapter 14

Date: _____

Things I need to do: _____

Notes:

Chapter 15:
Executive Summary

The summary for your proposal is put at the beginning of the document but is written last. The summary is a clear one page abstract of the entire proposal. Most foundations and government funding sources request a summary.

Write one short paragraph explaining each element. Follow the order given below:

The summary has to be well written so that the reviewer will get a clear understanding of the need for your program or project and the expected results.

Be sure to write a compelling need statement that the program is addressing. Discuss the real problem and how your organization plans to resolve the problem. Show the funder the importance of your program. Write a persuasive summary to get the interest of the funder. The summary should be brief but very convincing. Mention the essential points of the proposal. DO NOT EXCEED ONE PAGE. Remember the summary is a brief document that captures the highlights of your total proposal.

A summary contains the following elements:

1. Identification of the applicant
2. The specific purpose of the grant
3. Qualifications to carry out the purpose
4. The anticipated end result
5. The amount of money requested
6. The total program or project budget.

NOTES: Chapter 15

Date: _____

Things I need to do: _____

Notes:

Chapter 16:
Submitting Your Proposal to the Funder

In preparation for submitting your finished proposal to a funder the proposal should be clean and neatly packaged. The proposal should be free of any wrinkles, stains, or undesirable spots. If the proposal is neatly and professionally packaged it gives the impression of a well organized successful organization. The preparation and presentation says a lot for the organization. Follow the guidelines of the funder for submitting your proposal in the format of how the proposal should be put together. Make sure all assurances and certifications have been signed by the Executive Director or the person who is legally authorized by the organization to sign legal documents. Do not add photographs, charts, or graphs unless they are required by the funder. If these items are required, be sure to include them. Make sure your proposal pages are numbered according to the RFP guidelines or other funder requirements.

Once the proposal is complete make sure at least three people in the organization reviews it for accuracy and content. If there are any errors they should be corrected before the final draft goes to the Executive Director for final review. Once the Executive Director views the proposal and feels that everything is in order, the proposal is now ready to go to official print and prepared for the Executive Director's signature as well as any other signatures that are required by the funder. All signatures must be official hand written signatures in black ink. The RFP will usually state black or blue ink, but it is usually black ink for signatures. Do not use red ink for signatures. Black or blue ink is preferred for copy purposes. Black or blue ink can be seen easier when documents are photocopied. Red ink is hard to see when photocopied. Never use a **rubber stamp** for original signatures on a grant proposal. A rubber stamp is not usually an acceptable signature. Follow the guidelines of the grant application for acceptable forms of signature(s).

If the proposal is hand delivered to the funder, ask the funder for a receipt. The receipt will show the date and time the proposal was delivered to the funder along with the signature of the person that accepted the proposal. If your organization utilizes the services of a mail system such as FedEx or UPS to pick up your proposal they both will give a receipt upon pick up from your organization. The receipt will have a tracking number if you need to correspond with them concerning the delivery of your proposal. The receipt will have a date and time on it. Both of these mailing services can guarantee when a letter or package can reach its destination.

If you choose to mail the proposal through a local post office, it is recommended that you mail the proposal at least 5 working days before the proposal is due. If you mail the proposal a little early, it will allow any delay that may be the result of the post office such as weekends, holidays, or even bad weather. Send the proposal by **CERTIFIED MAIL** with return receipt requested, **REGISTERED MAIL**, or **OVERNIGHT EXPRESS**. However, sending it overnight express can be risky. Your proposal still may not reach the funder by the deadline hour. It may reach the funder by the deadline day, but may not reach the funder by the right hour. If the deadline for the proposal is April 1, 2010 by 12:00 noon, but your proposal does not reach the funder until April 1, 2010 at 3:00 p.m. your proposal will be too late to be considered for funding because the cut off was 12:00 noon. Your proposal will be discarded.

If you are going to send your proposal overnight express, be sure to let the post office know that you need a guarantee delivery time. Ask the postal agent what time of day will your proposal reach the funding agency? Pay close attention to the date and hour your proposal is due to the funder. Mark your calendar as a reminder. The post office or other mailing services such as FedEx or UPS can let you know if your proposal can be delivered to the funder in time for the due date and time. It is imperative that your proposal reach the funder by the exact date and time set forth in the grant application. Sometimes the funder will give an extension for receiving grant proposals due to certain circumstances. The funder will notify all of the organizations that have sent in letters of intention to apply for funding. Each organization will be notified of the date and time of extension at the same time. The organizations may be notified by the funder of the extension by telephone, an official letter, or by the internet website. Mark your calendar for the new date and time to submit your grant proposal to the funder. You can also call the funder to verify the extension of the new date and time for submitting your grant proposal.

It's a chance you take when you wait until the last minute to mail a proposal. Be sure to get a receipt from the post office and a tracking number so you can follow up on the delivery of your proposal if you need to. Your receipt is the only proof you will have that you mailed your proposal. Keep your mailing receipt in a safe place with a copy of your proposal. After you have mailed your proposal, give the postal system or the delivery company you used to mail the proposal a chance for your proposal to travel. After a sufficient amount of travel time for the proposal to arrive at its destination, you may contact the funder by telephone to ask if they have received your proposal. You can also go on the internet and track your proposal by the tracking number that you were provided with when you mailed your proposal. Make sure you mail your proposal by a means of knowing how to confirm that your proposal did in fact reach the funder in time.

If your proposal is a government proposal, the RFP will state how many copies to send along with the original proposal. Foundations and other funders will give you their guidelines for submitting a proposal. Some government agencies will ask for **ONE ORIGINAL and FIVE**

COPIES. Be sure to differentiate the original proposal from the copies. You can write the word original on the front cover of the original and mark copies on the cover of each copy. You can also use a rubber stamp that says original or copy. These stamps can be purchased at any stationery store. Do not send any more proposals than is requested. The reason a funder may request as many as 5 copies is for the benefit of the proposal review committee members. They each need their own copy. With technology media today, the funder might request that you submit the grant proposal on a computer disc (CD). If so, send the proposal on a CD as requested.

The funder will state in the guidelines how they want the proposal packaged. They will want all of the pages numbered in sequence. The RFP will state how the table of contents should be presented.

The cover page should give the name of the organization, the name of the program or project, the date of submission, the name of the funder, the name of the contact person for your organization, and the program or project number.

If the funder is a governmental agency the program or project RFP will have a number assigned to the announcement. Put this number on the cover page so the funder can identify what RFP you are responding to. Governmental agencies send out several RFP's at the same time. Therefore, they need to know what announcement your organization is applying for funding. For example, if the State Department of Health has an RFP circulating announcing a Teen Pregnancy Prevention Program, the RFP number might be T00.0005. This is the number that will identify your proposal once it is received by the funder's office. There can be another RFP circulating for A Domestic Abuse Education Program in which that program could have the RFP number D555.000. Both proposals would have to be separated by name and number. If you had a reason to call the funder to ask a question about a proposal, the funder would ask you what the number on the announcement is. The number serves as an identification number to the RFP. Some funders use only the name of the program.

Foundations or corporations do not use numbers to identify their projects. You need only put the name of the proposed program or project on the cover page and this is sufficient. Foundations and corporations can give you their guidelines for submitting proposals to them. They have different requirements from governmental agencies.

Remember to watch out for major holidays when mail is not delivered Mail the proposal before the holidays if the proposal is due around a holiday. For example, if a proposal is due on November 27th which is usually close to Thanksgiving, mail the proposal on November 21st. Also consider the weekends when mail is not delivered. Mailing your proposal on a Saturday when it is due on Monday just two days away is too close to chance. Even though you mailed the proposal on Saturday, mail is not delivered on Sunday, therefore, it might reach the funder on Monday by the due date but might be too late in terms of the hour it is due. Don't take this risk! You must also take into consideration that the governmental agencies are large establishments with large mail rooms. If your proposal is mailed where thousands of pieces of mail are delivered every day, your proposal can sit in a stack for several days while the mail is being sorted in the mail room. Your proposal should be at least post marked by the deadline date. Governmental agencies will usually honor proposals that are postmarked by the deadline date. The postmark must be done by a United States Postal Service, not an organization's own postal meter.

Remember to pay close attention to the deadline date for proposal submissions. **Funders do not except any excuses for late proposals.** The proposal is disqualified if it is received in the funder's office late. The grant proposal process is extremely competitive. If your proposal arrives late you are out of luck for having your proposal considered for funding.

EXTENSIONS GRANTED BY THE FUNDER:

In some circumstances the funder will send out a request for proposal (RFP) RFP where there is not enough turnaround time for the organization to write a proposal and get it back to the funder by the initial due date. If enough grant seekers call the funder to voice their concerns about not having enough time to write a good proposal, the funder will send out an addendum which will extend the application process due date. The funder will announce an extension date on the same RFP. Your organization will receive written notification of this extension. If you do not receive written notification, the funder will make a telephone call to your organization notifying of the extension. This new extension date will supersede the first announcement date. The new date is what you will work towards. You can call the funder to confirm the new extension date if you have questions of the correct submission deadline date. Be sure to get the **new date and time** the proposal is due in the funders office. The extension can be at least two –three weeks. Extensions rarely go over a thirty day timeframe. You will want to mark your calendar for the new date the proposal is due to the funder. Only one extension is usually granted on the same grant proposal application.

Be sure to use your check list to make sure you have submitted all materials requested by the funder. Check off each item that you have completed. Have someone on the proposal writing team to double check for all certifications and assurances and all other legal documents that need to be submitted with the proposal. Have at least 3 people review your proposal before it is submitted to the funder. Check for accuracy, format, content, and quality. Proof and edit the final document.

Be sure to follow the RFP guidelines or grant application. Use your checklist to make sure you have submitted all materials requested by the funder. Check off each item that you have completed. Have another person on the grant writing team double check the checklist to make sure all of the requirements have been met.

Packaging your proposal:

Send the original and copies in one package. Be sure to mark the original document with the word "**original**" and mark the copies with the word "**copies**". If the funder is requesting CD's or DVDs" with the proposal, be sure to include the disc with the proposal in the same packaging with the original and copies of the written documents. Include the amount of CD' or DVD's that are requested. A proposal can be denied funding for not including a CD or DVD if it is requested by the funder and they are not included.

Do not separate the original proposal document from the copies. The proposal must arrive to the funder intact with all of the materials in the same package together. If the original is separated from the copies, this could cause confusion for the review team. The proposal could get logged in twice. It could be read twice and ranked twice by a different team of readers. There may be as many as five to seven people on the review panel. Each reviewer will need to have a full proposal package of your materials. That is the reason why the funder will ask for one original and several copies of your proposal. This will insure that everyone serving on the review panel will have their own copy as the proposals are being reviewed for possible funding. The proposal will automatically be disqualified for funding if the proposal is not complete and in order. It is imperative that the proposal is submitted all together in the same box or envelope.

Before mailing or hand delivering your proposal, make sure you have met all of the requirements for submitting a successful grant proposal. Mail your proposal in plenty of time to reach the funder. Get a receipt showing proof of mailing from your postal carrier.

See the sample proposal checklist on the following pages.

Sample Proposal Checklist

The RFP Application will give the guidelines for submitting the proposal

Name of proposed project or program: _____

Name of Funder or Donor: _____

Be sure to check the following before submitting your final proposal:

Follow the guideline requirements received from the funder
A thorough outline of the funder's requirements for the proposal content has been written and double-checked by 3 people.
All RFP application guidelines has been followed as required
Include all Memorandum of Understandings (MOU) and Memorandum of Agreements (MOA)
Show research to support your problem statement
Show research to support your proposed methodology to address the problem statement. Discuss your approach
Discuss support of the expected results on successful completion of your project
Identified key personnel to work on the project. Attach Bio's or resume's for each employee. Make sure all personnel have the qualifications for their position.
Attach appropriate letters of support for your project or program.
Inc-lude documentation of arrangements with partnerships. Attach involvement documentation. What will the partners contribute to the project or program?
Attach tax status letter, annual report, annual budget summary, insurance policies, have appropriate people sign all certificates, assurances, all legal documents required by the funder
Attach the entire budget including itemization of expenses.
Explanation of what items are being supplied by your organization and what items are being contributed or donated by other organizations.
The problem statement is written with clarity. Describe the problem. What is the cause? What is the need?

Sample Proposal Checklist Continued:

The "Vision" statement is written with clarity.
You have listed the short term goals of the project or program
You have listed the long terms goals.
You have stated your objectives for what you hope to accomplish.
You have included a dissemination plan for your project or program.
Your evaluation plan is written and attached.
The sustainability plan is written and attached. You have discussed your continuation plan for your program or project.
The introduction is attached.
The project or program summary is attached.
The executive summary is well written with clarity.
The table of contents is attached per guidelines of the RFP if required.
Include the Title page. Follow the format of the funder if one is provided.
Include the cover letter. Have the appropriate person sign it. A hand written signature is required in black or blue ink.
All forms have been completed and appropriate signature(s) are obtained. All original signatures are in black or blue ink. Signature may include the CEO, CFO, Chairperson of the Board of Directors, department heads, etc.
The Appendix is completed.
A draft of the entire proposal is proofed for grammar, spelling, and format and is reviewed by at least 3 people.
Where errors were identified, corrections and revisions were made to the final draft.
The cover letter is included with the appropriate signature(s) obtained.
The master original proposal is printed in its entirety. Supplemental materials or other documentation are included.
Follow the guidelines of the RFP or grant application. If the applications request sending one original and a certain number of copies be sure to send the correct number of copies with the original. Mark one copy original and mark the others with the word copies. You can divide the copies with a separate sheet of paper in between each copy. Also include computer CD disk or DVD if it is requested of the funder. Send correct number of CD's disk as requested.
The proposal is put together in accordance with the guidelines of the funder.
Make sure you include the correct number of copies as requested by the funder. Send in the format requested, for example, hard paper copy and/or CD or compact disk.
Use the checklist packaged in the RFP if required. Package the proposal by the guidelines of the funder.
Check the table of contents for page accuracy. Make sure all pages are in the correct order by the funders requirements.

All forms have been completed and appropriate signature(s) obtained. All original signatures are in black or blue ink.
Check the RFP if the proposal should be bound or unbound. Follow all the required guidelines of the funder regarding how to submit your proposal
Type a clear shipping label with the correct mailing address of the funder. If the proposal is shipped in a box, make sure the proposal is protected from getting damaged in the box. Pack the proposal so as to not damage the edges. Do not allow the proposal to shift while in the box. Secure the proposal by packing it securely.
Print the name of the funder on the shipping label. Print the name of the contact person you are sending your proposal to. Be sure to put your organizations return address on the label.
Mail your proposal in enough time to reach the funder by the deadline. Allow enough time for the proposal to travel and arrive on time. Call the funder to find out if the funder has received your proposal. Send proposal by certified mail. Get a receipt showing proof of mailing of your proposal.
If the proposal can be hand delivered, deliver the proposal at least one week before it is due if possible. This will ensure that your proposal has been received by the funder by the deadline date and time.
The proposal should be presented as required by the guidelines of the funder. The proposal should be written in the right font type size, page numbers, margins, right paper size, on white paper, etc. Each page number should be in order including forms. Each page should be neat and clean. Do not use white-out on any page. The paper must be free of stains, spots, smudges.etc. Any art work, graphics, charts, diagrams, or photographs should be clear and easy to read.
Complete all forms in the grant application or the RFP. Do not leave any questions blank or unanswered. If a question does not apply to your organization, write "Not applicable". This lets the funder know that you did read or see the question. It just didn't apply to your organization.

> Date that you mailed or delivered the master original proposal and required copies per funder requirement. Date shipped: _____
>
> Time: _____
>
> Date hand delivered to funder: _____
>
> Time: _____
>
> Be sure to keep copies of the proposal for your organization in a safe place. This proposal copy should be maintained in a safe place within your organization. This includes all forms and a computer disk of the proposal. This can be a bound copy, a non-bound hard copy, or a compact disk (CD). Also maintain the receipts you received when you mailed your proposal to the funder. Send the proposal by certified mail or hand deliver on time. Organize and file all drafts of any proposals written. Be sure to put dates on each draft. Label each draft by name of proposal and number the version. For example draft #1, Lock the proposals in a safe area.

NOTES: Chapter 16

Date: _____

Things I need to do: _____

Notes:

Chapter 17:
Funder's Decision

After the funding agency has received and reviewed all proposals that met the requirements for funding, the review committee will assign each proposal a score. The proposals are given 0-100 points. This has been discussed in the evaluation chapter. The proposals that receive the highest score will be recommended for funding. Once it has been determined which organization will be funded, that organization will be sent a written notice or letter telling the organization that their proposal was selected for funding. It usually takes about 4-6 weeks to hear a decision from the funder. It could be less or more time. This is a time where you will have to have patience. You will be notified in one way or the other as soon as a decision is made. You will not have to contact the funder. They will contact the Executive Director of the organization. However, if you don't hear anything in about 4 weeks you can call to find out the status of your proposal. The funder will let you know the process.

WHEN THE PROJECT or PROGRAM IS SELECTED FOR FUNDING:

When the organization's project or program is funded, the funder and the organization's representative will both sign a contract which is exactly like the proposal. The contract will give the organization all of the rules and regulations that will govern the operation of the proposed program or project. The organization that is selected for funding must adhere to all of the stipulations of the contract. If the organization fails to abide by the contract agreement the organization will be cited for being "out of contract compliance" which carries penalties or consequences for the organization.

Once the organization has been informed of the good news of being funded, the first thing the awarded organization should do is to immediately telephone the funding agency and say thank you. **A formal letter should be sent to express the organization's appreciation.** The organization should keep in touch with the funder. It is always nice to invite the funder to an event or to give the funder a tour of the facility if they have never had a tour. Once your newly funded program is up and running you can invite the funder to see a program in action. Be sure to introduce the funder to key staff in your organization during the tour.

Your organization has now established a professional relationship with the funder. It is important to nurture this relationship. You have worked very hard for this partnership. Establish a good line of communication with this funder.

The level of recognition for a grant should be proportionate to the amount of funds received. For example, a thank you letter may be sufficient for a small grant. However, a funder may donate one million or several million dollars to your organization. In this case, a building can be named after a big contributor. Some universities have buildings named in honor of a big donor. Medical centers are named after big donors. Again it depends on the amount of funding. These are usually large donations from the private sector. Another way of showing appreciation to a funder is to have a special event and honor the funder. The organization can write a press release to the media for public acknowledgement. The donor or funder can be honored at an annual event. A special luncheon can be held to honor donors no matter what the amount of the donation. The donors can be presented with a special plaque to say "thank you" for your contribution. There are many ways an organization can give recognition to a funder.

Whether the grant is small or large, recognition is always given to a funder. This is proper protocol. Keep in mind that whatever the funder has awarded small or large, the funder has shown support to your organization and program. Funders like to feel that they made the right decision to fund your program or project, therefore, always let the funder know how your program is progressing. From time to time send them testimonials or pictures of some of your activities.

If your organization is having any difficulties bring this matter to the attention of the funder as soon as possible so that the funder is aware and can possibly offer recommendations as to how to resolve the problems. Your program can run into problems that are beyond your organization's control. Your funders are human and understand that situations arise without any forewarning or prior knowledge. Your funder will work with you should you run into problems. After all, they have a vested interest in the organization and the program they have selected to fund. They want your program or project to be successful.

WHEN THE PROPOSAL IS NOT FUNDED: TURN YOUR NO into YES!

If your proposal was denied try not to get too upset. There is always another time to submit your proposal. There will be another funding cycle in which you can resubmit your proposal to the same funder. Once your organization is notified in writing that your proposal was not funded you can contact the funder. The letter you receive may be very vague and you may want more specific information as to why your proposal was denied for funding. You can ask the funder to give you a clear explanation as to the content of your proposal. Here are a few questions you can ask the funder or you may have others of your own. These are just some examples:

1. What kind of information was missing in the proposal?
2. What were some of the questions the reviewers had while they were reading the proposal?
3. What could have been stated with more clarity?
4. How could the proposal have been stronger?
5. What were the weak areas in the proposal?
6. How could the proposal been more competitive?
7. Did our organization follow the proposal guidelines?
8. Ask if your organization meets the criteria to resubmit the proposal?
9. When is the resubmission date?

The funder will let you know the reason why your proposal was not selected for funding. Pay close attention to the critique of your proposal. Find out what the weak points were. Ask the funder what you could have done to strengthen your proposal. You can continue to build a relationship with the funder in spite of the first denial. Who knows you might win on the second time around. Don't give up! Send your proposal to other perspective funders once you work out the rough edges of the proposal that was denied. Do whatever you can to make your proposal stronger.

Just a suggestion, if your organization has submitted the proposal to at least two different funding sources and they both denied the proposal it may be time to contact a professional grant writer. A professional grant writer has experience reading RFP's and funding announcements. A professional grant writer can read your proposal and offer some suggestions which might help to get your proposal funded. A professional grant writer will look at your proposal with a critical eye and will be able to analyze some of the problem areas and offer recommendations for corrections. You can work along with a professional grant writer and brainstorm together and discuss strategies for improving your proposal.

Any grant proposal is subject to not being funded although the grant proposal is well written and all of the necessary documentation is included. You may have followed all of the guidelines and fulfilled all of the requirements included in the application. The proposal may have been delivered by the deadline on time. There is still no guarantee that the grant proposal will be funded. The grant application will be reviewed by professional experts in the field. The experts make up a committee of people not just one person. Each proposal will be reviewed extensively and rigorously. The review committee will determine whether or not a grant award will be made.

Appeal Process-

When an organization is denied funding but they feel they should have been awarded the grant instead of another agency, the organization that was denied can challenge the validity of the grant awarding process. They can ask for the scores of the rating sheets of other competitors and file an appeal if there is just cause. An appeal involves legal representation on both sides and can turn into a lengthy and costly process. The awarded agency will not get the funds until the appeal process is over. The funder still makes the final determination of who will be awarded the funds. Once the final decision is made at the conclusion of the appeal process, the funds will be released to the winning organization. The case is closed. The funds are released to the winning organization.

If you were not funded and the appeal process did not work in your favor, do not give up. Continue to write grant proposals and submit them to several different funding sources. Your determination and hard work will pay off! Some day you will receive a letter saying yes, to your proposal. Just don't give up!

NOTES: Chapter 17

Date: _____

Things I need to do: _____

_____
_____
_____
_____
_____
_____
_____

Notes:

_____
_____
_____
_____
_____
_____
_____
_____
_____
_____
_____
_____
_____
_____
_____
_____
_____
_____
_____
_____
_____
_____

Chapter 18:
Funding Resources

With the advancement of internet websites to disseminate information on nonprofit organizations, foundations, and other charity organizations, finding money to fund programs or projects, are little easier. The internet lists many foundations and corporations that donate money to many qualifying nonprofit organizations. A few years ago, I put together a list of funding resources for grant seekers, however some of the funding sources that were available at that time are no longer active. Therefore, I felt it would be best to provide you with the resources via the internet so that you may search for funding sources on your own. The information on the internet can change, at any given time. However, it is currently the best and most effective way to do research for your funding needs. There is a wealth of information on the internet about funding resources on foundation directories and foundation centers.

Foundation funding:

Definition of a foundation: A foundation is a legal categorization of nonprofit organizations that will typically either donate funds and support to other organizations, or provide the source of funding for its own charitable purposes. (Wikipedia.org). It is a "nongovernmental entity that is established as a nonprofit corporation or a charitable trust, with a principal purpose of making grants to unrelated organizations, institutions, or individuals for scientific, educational, cultural, religious, or other charitable purposes. There are two foundation types: private foundations and grant making public charities. A private foundation derives its money from a family, an individual, or a corporation. A grant making public charity derives its support from diverse sources, which may include foundations, individuals, and government agencies. (http://foundationcenter.org. 2010)

There are several grant funding resources available to grant seekers. Research can be done via the internet or public libraries for funding resources. A grant seeker can seek information from the foundation directory which is an excellent resource for researching funding for your organization. You can look at private 501(c)(3) nonprofit foundations. There are hundreds of foundations around this nation that provide substantial amount of funding to nonprofit organizations whose interest matches the interest of the grant funder. The mission of foundations is to provide funding for a particular cause or to support community programs or project for which the foundation was founded.

Foundation Centers:

The Foundation Center is an independent nonprofit information clearing house established in 1956. The center's mission is to foster public understanding of the foundation filed by collecting, organizing, and disseminating information on foundations, corporate giving and related subjects. (Burke & Prater 2000)

I spent two full days at the Foundation Center in Atlanta, Georgia researching monies for education, health, social services for the elderly population, youth and teen programs. I found the librarian to be extremely helpful in my search for funding in these categories. The Foundation center contains volumes of collections of material on philanthropy. It is open to the public and free of charge. You will need to plan a full day or more to have sufficient time to research the category of funding you are looking for. You don't want to be in a rush when you go to the foundation center library. It will take some time just to get oriented to the center and to locate the information you are seeking. During my visit to the library I was able to obtain grant making materials. I was provided with annual reports, and corporate giving reports in the categories for which I was seeking funding.

The foundation center did offer grant writing workshops for grant seekers. The foundation center will have information for the public to inform people as to when the foundation will be offering a grant writing class. The grant writer will need to identify the foundation center location in their respective state and inquire at that foundation about any upcoming grant writing workshops. The grant seeker will need to ask if there is a charge to attend the workshop? If there is a charge for the workshop, it will be money well spent for the knowledge and information you will learn from an expert in the field of grant writing. The information the grant seeker will receive will help in the planning and development of writing and submitting a successful grant application or proposal.

There are volumes of books on philanthropy giving at the foundation center. I was able to gain a lot of valuable information of where and how to get funding for specific projects or programs. Each foundation will state their mission and their interest as to what types of grants the foundation is interested in funding. The foundations directories list the name of the foundation, the contact person to get in touch with regarding funding, the funding cycle or dates of when the foundation gives out grant money, and what types of grants and the amount of award money that is given to a particular nonprofit organization. Most of the foundation awards are given to nonprofit organizations. However, some foundations may also give money to individuals such as educational scholarships to students for example. With today's technology and access to the internet, a grant seeker can access a foundation center website and gain information about a foundation anytime of the day or night.

Community Foundations:

Community foundations are nonprofit. This is considered a public charity. "These foundations focus on the community in which they are located" (New & Quick1998). Their focus is to raise money from the general public. Community foundations provide funding to programs and projects that benefit communities. They offer more control over their charitable giving. http://en.wikipedia.org (2010).

Government funding:

Government funding is different from foundation funding. Government funding is derived from tax payer dollars. The United States government spends millions and billions of dollars funding projects or programs from research and development, obtaining facilities, renovation or refurbishing facilities, to economic development projects, to funding social service agencies which will meet the needs of communities. The government funds an array of educational institutions private or public. Churches are eligible for funding under the "Christian-initiative based funding resources. Medical facilities, programs, and projects are funded by the USA federal government. Colleges, universities, and technical schools public and private are funded by the federal government. Financial aid to college students are awarded by the federal government. Funding all of these programs, projects, institutions, and building facilities can equate into billions of dollars annually. The government also funds disaster relief projects which can provide substantial help to people faced with an immediate crisis without any warning. When a grant seeker looks to the federal government for funding they must be ready for the challenge. The competition for federal grants is very intense and stiff. When the government mails out a notice of funds availability (NOFA), these notices go out to all nonprofit as well as some for-profit businesses to apply for funding that has been announced in the grant proposal request for proposal (RFP). Every organization who has an interest in the project that is being announced in the RFP will apply for this round of funding. Not every proposal will be funded. Federal grant proposals can be very tedious and time consuming. I know because I have first hand experience in writing federal grant proposals. I have written many. You must stay focused and not take anything for granted. Timing is of the essence for a federal grant proposal.

The grant seeker will need to be very organized. Federal grants can be in the amounts of millions of dollars for one project or social programs which ever applies to your organization. If the grant amount is in the millions of dollars and your organization has adequate staffing, it is strongly recommended that the organization applying for funding have a grant writing team who is trained, and has experience in writing federal grant proposals.

The proposal has to be written with clarity as to its mission, goals, and objectives. Sometimes an organization will seek the assistance for a technical support person to consult or get help in writing the grant application or proposal. When the grant amounts are in the million dollar range, the funds are usually ear marked for a period of several years, at least three to four years has been my experience. Some funding periods may be longer or shorter. The RFP will state how long the funding period will last. Be sure to read the RFP very carefully. Follow the instructions and guidelines perfectly. Make sure your organization has the authority by the appropriate individual(s) to apply for federal funding. An authorized person such as the chairperson on the board of directors or the organizations CEO has the authority to apply for the funding. Sometimes a letter of intent to apply for funding is required. The letter of intent is a letter written to inform the federal agency that your organization plans to apply for the funding stated in the "notice of funding availability (NOFA) or the RFP. The letter of intent must also be signed by an authorized person of the organization.

Make sure you apply for the specific project or activity that is announced in the RFP or NOFA document. For example, if the NOFA or RFP is announcing funding for an "early childhood development center" in a low income community, don't submit a proposal for a senior citizen high rise complex. Most federal RFP's will have a project number to identify the name of the project that the government is seeking grant proposals for. Lastly, make sure your organization is eligible to apply for this funding. If you are not sure if your organization is eligible for this funding, call the funder and ask who is eligible for funding?

State department funding:

Funding from your local State department is also tax payer based. The funding is derived from tax payers of the state where the organization is located. State funding is provided to educate public school systems, medical institutions, construct or maintain facilities, law enforcements agencies, social service programs to meet the needs of individuals, families, and communities, and many other areas of interest. It has been my experience that state grants were much more competitive than federal grants. (Burke and Prater 2000) explains that "competition for state grants tends to be more severe than federal grants because people are more familiar with their local agency and can often solicit help from local school or government offices." State department grants are just as tedious as federal grant proposals. Again, there are hundreds of nonprofit organizations applying for the same funding you are seeking. The federal and state government must be responsible and accountable with its funding of programs or projects. Therefore your program or project must be in line with and be eligible for the funding that is announced in the RFP's

The state department will sometimes offer nonprofit organization the opportunity to attend a bidder's conference. The bidder's conference is a conference sponsored by the awarding state agency where the nonprofit organization is located. The funder will let the grant seeker know if and when a bidder's conference is going to be held. The advantage of attending a bidder's conference is to allow the grant seeker to meet the funder and to ask any questions they may have on the grant application. Word of caution! Don't be late for the bidder's conference. They usually begin on time. If you arrive late to the bidder's conference you will risk missing some vital information that is provided by the funder. The funder will go through the grant application process and answer questions from anyone in attendance. You will have an opportunity to share any concerns you may have about the application process. There is a period of time that you can call and ask the funder questions that you do not understand. Be sure to mail or deliver your application on time. If your proposal is delivered late you will be out of the competition for the funding. There are no exceptions! Everyone is on an equal playing field.

Corporations:

Corporations are a great resource for funding nonprofit organizations. Corporations will donate to nonprofit organizations which are usually community oriented. They want to have name recognition in their local areas. Corporations will form partnerships with school districts, churches, medical facilities such as hospitals, colleges and universities, just to name a few. Donations to a nonprofit organization will provide excellent exposure and public relations for the corporation. The corporation wants to be viewed as a positive force in the community. Contributions to a nonprofit organization will enhance the image of the corporation. The public will be more apt to even shop, trade, or do business at a particular business or establishment if it has earned the reputation of reaching out and giving back to communities. Corporations can provide many different resources to a nonprofit organization beside financial resources. Some corporations will lend their employees to nonprofit organizations during a special event such as a major fundraising to help raise money for a particular charity for example. Corporations will lend their expertise on a volunteer bases to nonprofit organizations such as a law firm can donate time and provide free legal consultation to a nonprofit organization.

It is much easier to seek funding from your regional or local corporations because they are usually closer to your organizations location. For example, a school can partner with a corporation and form a very long business and school partnership relationship. The school will draw up a partnership contract naming the school and the corporation now as partners. The corporation will provide money and other material resources to the school they have partnered with. Some corporations only require a simple 1-2 page letter from the grant seeking organization asking for funding for a particular project. Corporations will sometimes allocate funding for nonprofit organizations at special times during the year. For example, a corporation may make a donation to a nonprofit organization that wants to provide food for the homeless population during the Thanksgiving holidays. Some corporations have already designated nonprofit organizations to provide food for the homeless at Thanksgiving on an annual continuous basis. Contact your local or regional grocery chain food stores and continue to ask for food donations to feed hungry people for the Thanksgiving holidays. If you persevere you will get donations. If one food grocery chain turns you down, don't give up! Contact another grocery store. You will eventually get a food donation to feed homeless and hungry individuals. Be sure to write letters to grocery stores whose mission is to address the problem of hunger. A corporation's who's goal is to help eliminate hunger in low income communities will be more apt to make a financial donation to your organization because your are seeking funding for feeding hungry people which is a match for their interest.

Corporations will usually ask for your proof of a 501(c)(3) "determination letter" given by the IRS to make sure you are a nonprofit organization and are eligible to receive charitable contributions from corporations. When corporations make a donation to a nonprofit organization, their goal is to make a difference in a community. The corporation will benefit also because they are able to write off their contribution on the corporations income taxes. Therefore, the community and the corporation both benefit.

Contributions from other organizations and individuals:

There are charities, organizations, and individuals who also make financial contributions of various amounts to nonprofit organizations to improve the quality of life in communities. Local organizations also have a mission to fulfill. A grant seeker can research different social organizations on the internet. If a contact number is listed, you may want to call the organization and inquire about any funding possibilities or opportunities for funding.

Professional athletes make contributions to nonprofit organizations and various charities. Celebrities with name recognition and fame will participate in fund-raising events such as "Celebrity Telethons" to help raise funding for nonprofit organizations. Celebrities feel honored to help raise money for a specific cause that they are personally passionate about.

Private social organizations and individuals provide money for specific activities to help communities fulfill a need. There are sororities and fraternities at colleges and universities who offer community services to local students or residents. The sororities and fraternities often provide mentoring services, and tutorial services for students who need help academically. These organizations are very community oriented and are involved in many social activities for the betterment of mankind.

There are organizations that will help by planning and participating in a big fundraising event to raise money for a nonprofit organization.

Some companies will donate a product to a special event rather than money. For example, Haggen-Dazs Ice Cream Company donated a variety of their ice cream to a nonprofit organization I was employed with for the organization's "Community Unity Fun Day" event in California. Haggen –Dazs actually sent their ice cream truck to the site of the event. With the help of Haggen-Dazs ice cream, the event was a huge success. The children and adults truly enjoyed the varieties of ice cream donated by Haggen-Dazs. The grant seeker can send a letter to the contributions desk of a funder and inquire what product their company can donate to nonprofit organizations.

Church or Religious groups funding:

Churches or other religious organizations can make donations or contributions to other 501 (c)(3) organizations. Churches are considered a 501(c)(3) nonprofit public charity tax exempt organizations by the IRS. Finances for churches are derived from its members of the church and nonmembers. The church or other religious organizations may provide funding to community service organizations that provide services to specific causes and purposes that will benefit a target population and communities. Churches may provide funding for disaster relief programs, provide services to the poor and disadvantaged, for educational and religious programs or projects, to provide food for the hungry, and meets the social and economical needs of individuals of a community regardless of their membership status, cultural and ethnical backgrounds, gender or race. People see churches as a place of refuge. They turn to the church for help as a last resort. Churches can provide an array of services through outreach projects in a community. Most churches have a benevolent fund to help individuals or families in crisis. Churches are not required to pay income taxes on the monies that they receive from its members, visitors, or other outside contributors. Most of the churches income is non-taxable income. Therefore, grant seekers that are affiliated with other 501(c)(3) nonprofit organizations that are tax exempt by the IRS, can solicit funding from churches or other religious groups to help individuals in need, to provide emergency assistance when needed, to provide help to families in need, and sponsor special community events when needed for the betterment of the target population.

Anonymous donors:

There are individuals who will fund a program or project with a large endowment or donation and will ask to remain anonymous. This is usually done through private solicitation. Anonymous donors do not want their identity disclosed to the public. I had this experience when I founded a nonprofit organization in California to provide a drug and gang prevention program for at risk youth. Individuals were making donations to the organization and I never learned who the donors were.

One company created and designed all of my brochures and had them delivered to the organization anonymously. I could not thank who ever made the donations because the contributors wanted to remain anonymous. I felt very blessed for their contributions. Some individuals do not want to be acknowledged publically for contributions they make. If this happens in your organization where the donor or funder wants to remain anonymous you will want to respect their wishes as long as no laws are broken.

During the process of researching funders, the problem must be stated very clearly to the funder. The program or project must be well planned and developed with clear goals and objectives. The vision and mission must be clearly understood by the funder. The grant seeker needs to realize that writing grant proposals to various funders are very competitive. For example, if a governmental agency sends out a notice of funds availability (NOFA) to 100 nonprofit organizations that are addressing the problem of homeless high risk youth, and your organization is seeking funding to address the problem of homeless high risk youth, your organization is competing against 99 other nonprofit organizations for the same block of funding for their homeless high risk youth program. The competition can be fierce for these dollars. The same competition holds true for funding from private foundations and corporations.

Grants are awarded from several different sources. A nonprofit organization can apply for funding from the federal government, the State government, local city government, local county government, private foundations, public foundations, corporations, and companies. They all have different funding requirements and guidelines. The grant seeker will need to research to find out what each prospective funder requires to fund a program or project.

The grant seeker will need to identify the problem using the methods talked about in earlier chapters. Once the problem has been identified, the grant seeker will need to design a project or develop and plan a program that will be viable and reasonable to solve the problem. The grant seeker will need to research and identify funders who have an interest in addressing the same problem as the grant seeker for the organization. The goals, objectives, vision, mission, and purpose of the nonprofit organization must be a match for the funder.

Grant seekers can write several different program or project proposals for many different funders and have them on hand so when an RFP is announced for a program or project that is of interest to the organization and the funder, the grant writer will be in the position to submit the proposal by the deadline date. If the grant seeker is pro-active in writing grant proposals in hopes that a RFP will be announced in a funding cycle, the grant seeker will be ahead in the process.

Proposals for program or projects are extremely competitive no matter who the funder is. It doesn't matter if the funding is coming from the federal government, city, county, state, private foundations, corporations, and various local companies. Due to the fact that the funding process is very competitive, grant seeking is an on-going endeavor for most nonprofit organizations.

A nonprofit organization that has a good managerial staff will have a grant writing team on staff that will seek out grants on a continuous basis. The grant writing team is usually aware of grant funding cycles with most governmental agencies. Funding that is derived from the federal government, the state government, city or county government agencies are considered public funding because these funds are made available through tax payer dollars. Private funders are foundations, corporations, and other companies. The government agencies have different requirements to award funding to nonprofit organizations from private funders such as foundations and corporations or other businesses.

The grant seeker must always keep in mind that it is imperative that the organizations proposal for funding matches the problem of the funder to solve the problem being addressed in the proposal. For example, if the funder has a passion or an interest in solving the problem of hunger in low income families, or addressing the problem of illiteracy among adults, you will not write and submit a proposal on an early childhood development center. You will want to write and submit a grant proposal to solve the problem of hunger among low income families. Your proposal will discuss how funding your proposal to solve the problem of hunger in a low income family and community will decrease or eliminate hunger in low income families and communities.

Or the grant seeker will address how the proposal being submitted for funding will address the problem of illiteracy among adults. Both the organization and the funder must be interested in solving the same problem. The funder wants to believe they are making a worthwhile investment in the organization and that the funding will benefit the target population and community for which the funding is being sought.

The organization must meet all of the necessary legal requirements and have the proper documentation to be eligible to receive funding from government or private sources. The nonprofit organization must be a 501(c)(3) tax exempt organization. This is a legal requirement for all nonprofit organizations.

When the grant seeker is researching funding sources, there is usually a telephone contact number listed by the funder where a grant seeker can call the funder and ask questions regarding eligibility requirements to receive funding. The funder will have their eligibility policy requirements in writing and may be able to fax or mail the grant seeker the grant application with eligibility requirements or the funder can gain information on the funding eligibility requirements on the internet. A grant seeker can access thousands of private funders which include foundations, government agencies, local agencies, companies, and corporations that fund nonprofit organizations on the internet at various websites. Researching funders can be very time consuming, but it will pay off if the grant seeker knows exactly what kind of funder they are looking for.

Match your grant proposal interest with the interest of the funder:

If a funder supports education it does not mean the funder will support any kind or all forms of education. The funder may only fund projects or programs that support early childhood education programs for children preK- grade 1. Therefore, a grant seeker would not submit a proposal to a funder if the organization is seeking funding to support a college scholarship program at a university even though it falls in the category of education. In this scenario, the funder would look for proposals that will educate young children preK-grade 1 only. Again, the proposal must match the interest of the funder as well as the organization seeking funding. The grant seeker will receive a rejection letter from the funder if there is no match in the specific category of level of education. There must be a match in interest for the funder and the nonprofit organization. The key to the grant seeker is finding a funder who shares the same interest as the organization.

Location:

Some requests for proposals (RFP) are announced in specific demographic areas. This is called a "catchment area". Announcements for funding are made in cities and counties very close to where the programs or projects are needed for the funding.. The grant seeker when researching funds for projects or programs must pay close attention to the location where the funder awards grant money. Funds can be awarded outside of a catchment area. Funders select the location where they want to fund projects or programs. The City or County agencies usually fund programs or projects where the nonprofit organization is located. This is local funding. Each State department funds programs or projects within the State of the proposed project or program usually using State funding. The federal government can fund programs or projects anywhere in the United States or internationally. The US government can fund projects or programs where justified. Private corporations will fund special projects or programs when and where they choose. Some corporations or companies will fund special projects or programs at specific times of the year. For example, a major food grocery store chain may donate food to feed the hungry at a homeless shelter during Thanksgiving holidays. Many companies and corporations lend a helping hand during a holiday season. These grocery stores are usually local within the community.

With the technology of computers and the internet, a grant seeker can access thousands of foundations, corporations, and governmental agencies to seek funding for a worthy cause to solve a variety of problems. The grant seeker must remember to match the nonprofit organizations problem with the problem of the funder.

Research for funding resources via the internet for nonprofit organization includes foundation centers, charitable grants, foundation grants, and nonprofit directory databases, foundations that give grants to Christian organizations called Christian grants, public libraries in all states, corporation grants, and government funding. The grant seeker can also access fundraising directories via the internet.

Be creative with your funding search:

As a grant writer, I have spent numerous hours at a foundation center. I gained a wealth of knowledge about funding possibilities. If you are willing to put the time into researching foundations, corporate sponsorships, public funding from the federal government, the state department, city government, county government, you will find funding for your program or project. You can also seek funding from for-profit businesses such as local banks, insurance companies, grocery store food chains, department stores, stationary stores, copy centers, and any other business who believe in your program or project.

Some corporations or companies are now donating gift cards instead of money. You can make a wish list of what your organization needs and present it to a funder. Locate a funder that provides the items that you are in need of. Once you submit a letter to the funder that can provide the items that you need, the company will decide if they want to donate money or a gift card. The company will put a designated amount on the gift card to allow the organization to use the card to purchase items listed on the wish list. This is the experience that I had last year. I submitted a letter on behalf of a church nonprofit organization asking for donations of food to feed individuals and families for the Thanksgiving holiday. The food company asked me for the church 501(c)(3) tax-exempt status "determination letter" provided by the Internal Revenue Service (IRS) showing proof of being a church nonprofit organization. I presented the documents requested by the food company. Upon review of the documents presented, the major food company donated gift cards to the organization to purchase food instead of sending a check. The church organization was very thankful for the gift cards. The organization was able to feed several families for the holiday season.

This is where the grant writer becomes very creative and thinks out of the box. You will be surprised as to where you can receive funding for your grant proposals. As mentioned earlier, even though you may not receive financial funding, you can receive contributions for your program or project for materials, for example, office supplies such as paper goods, office furniture can be donated from a furniture company, department stores can donate clothing for a clothing bank to provide clothing to the needy, printing companies can provide copies for flyers, computer companies can donate computers to a nonprofit organization who want to teach adults computer skills, just to name a few. Always be reasonable with your request for funding. Don't ask for more than what the funder has to offer.

I can't stress enough how important it is that the grant seeker matches the organizations interest with the interest of the funder. This is half the battle. Make sure your grant application or proposal is in line with the funders' vision, mission, goals, and objectives. If you are a match with the funder you will increase your chances of getting funding. As you search funding resources on the internet or from other leads to possible funding, make a list of those funders who you feel will be the most interested in your grant proposal. Call the funder if it is a foundation or a corporation, and discuss your proposal ideas with the funder. This is the first step.

If the funder expresses an interest in your grant proposal, ask the funder if it would be possible to meet with the individuals who are the decision makers of the foundation or corporation? If a meeting is arranged to meet with the funders, respect their time. Do not be late to the meeting. Arrive on time. Give a good first time impression. You are selling yourself and the organization you represent. Dress in appropriate business attire. Tell a compelling story as to why you need the funding, but do not beg. This will turn off the funder. Be prepared to answer any question the funder may ask about your proposal. Be open and honest with your answers to their questions. Be convincing and persuasive. Research the funder before you meet with the decision makers. Be knowledgeable in the event they ask you questions about their company and funding criteria.

At the conclusion of the meeting, thank the funders for giving you the opportunity to meet with them to discuss your proposal, and that you will appreciate them considering your proposal for funding. If your proposal has the interest of the funder, you may have a very good chance of getting funding.

Conclusion

It was my goal to provide a guide to beginner grant proposal writers in a basic simplistic manner. I hope this book is beneficial to you as you begin your journey in the field of professional grant proposal writing for nonprofit organizations. As I stated earlier in this book, grant writing is an art, it's technical, and a skill. It is also very competitive. It takes a lot of practice to become proficient at grant writing. You must have patience. This is not a skill you can learn over night. It takes time to master the craft.

You have to be determined to learn how to write successful grant proposals. It requires creativity, vision, and passion. Grant writers have an opportunity to pull on their own strengths, talents, and abilities to convey what they want to do to enhance people's lives through offering quality social service programs and projects to people and communities in need.

A glossary of grant terminology with definitions has been provided to help the grant writer understand the terminology that is used in writing grant proposals.

I offered recommendations and suggestions that would assist the beginner grant writer with skills to write a successful grant proposal. As a grant writer, you must stay focused on the "vision and mission" of the organization. Tell the funder how the organization is going to accomplish its mission. Write the grant proposal with clarity. Write compelling persuasive reason(s) to the funder regarding the need for funding. Assure the funder that the organization will carry out all of the program activities and services that are promised in your grant proposal, and that it is the organizations goal to continue its programs and services in the future.

Funders expect all grant recipients to deliver programs and services to their target population and communities with the highest level of integrity and abide by best practices of this industry.

Funders also want to believe that they have made a worthwhile investment in your organization and the community. Therefore, you want to exceed the funder's expectations by delivering programs and services with the highest degree of commitment, integrity, and professionalism.

Remember to stay focused on your vision, mission, goals and objectives. Be sure to match your interest with the interest of the funder. Do not ask for funding that exceeds the funders' amount a funder is willing to give.

Make sure your organization is eligible to apply for the specific funding. If you are awarded funding, remember to send an acknowledgement of a "thank you note". Show the funder you appreciate them for their belief in your proposed project or program.

Also remember, when a funder makes the decision to fund your grant proposal, the funder is investing in your organization's vision and mission. Go beyond the call of duty. Work in the spirit of excellence. The funder and the people in the communities you are proposing to help using the funding are counting on having a real problem solved.

Always follow the guidelines and instructions stated in the RFP or grant application. The organization needs to be aware of compliance issues and adhere to all contractual agreements.

See the vision! Write the vision! Do the vision! Enjoy the journey! Dreams do come true!

Additional Notes

Date: _____

Things I need to do: _____
_____
_____
_____
_____
_____
_____
_____

Notes:

_____
_____
_____
_____
_____
_____
_____
_____
_____
_____
_____
_____
_____
_____
_____
_____
_____
_____
_____
_____
_____

Appendix:
Glossary/Grant Terminology

Proposals consist of phrases and terminology that grant writers use. A glossary has been provided to assist you in learning proposal vocabulary. I have added some of my own. All of the terms are not used in this book. All funders are familiar with these terms and phrases. You should be able to demonstrate to the funder your understanding of proposal grant terminology.

Authorized agent/representative – an individual designated by the organization to sign legal documents such as applications for funding.
Authorizing signature – the organization representative(s) who must grant authority or power to submit application with all its assurances, guidelines, and restrictions.
Award – A grant.
Award Notice – formal written notification from a funding agency to a recipient applicant announcing that a grant has been awarded; also called "Notice of grant award".
Awarding agency – funding agency that makes a grant
Benchmarks – reference points for funders and fundees to assure that everything is on track.
Benefits – things that promote or enhance well-being; advantages.
Bidder's list – a list of qualified organizations maintained by government agencies for the purpose of sending potential bidders' invitations to submit proposals or bids on government contracts. Lists of bidders are used in determining to whom to send RFP's.
Bidders' conference – gathering to train and/ or explain the guidelines and concerns of a funding agency; usually held by government agencies after the application packets have been released to the public.
Block grant – a grant from a government funding source made as a total amount on the basis of some formula to a number of different recipients, often with relatively little control over its utilization; Revenue-sharing grants for certain general purposes are regarded as block grants.
Boilerplate – standard proposal sections that are used repeatedly in different contracts or proposals; includes staff resumes, descriptions of the school district student population, descriptions of the community, and identification of district resources and facilities.

Budget – itemized list of expenditures and income that accompanies a narrative proposal; a line-item summary of program revenues and expenses.
Budget Period – periods of time (usually twelve months) into which a project is divided for budget and reporting purposes; usually a continuation proposal is required each year that the project continues.
Building/renovation funds – money to build a new facility or renovate an existing facility; these projects are often referred to as bricks-and-mortar projects.
Capital outlay – tools, equipment, or apparatus purchased by the fundee for project implementation.
Capital support – money for equipment, buildings, construction, and endowments.
Capitation – payment per capita; used for a grant made to an organization on the basis of a given amount for each person enrolled or served, or potentially available to be served; the total amount of such a grant is the per capita amount granted multiplied by the number of persons served.
Categorical funding – most commonly refers to funds or projects limited to a specific educational purpose as opposed to general aid applicable to any school cost (examples: funds for educating handicapped students or another specific group and funds for specified programs such as vocational education).
Catchment – Demographic area for project or services (boundaries)
Circular A-110 – Office of Management and Budget (OMB) circular that sets forth the federal standards for financial-management systems to be maintained by organizations receiving federal funds.
Clearinghouse – state or local agency designated to review applications for funds in accordance with government regulations; see application guidelines to determine whether clearinghouse review is required.
Co-mingling of funds – taking money from one grant to cover expenditures for another project or activity; mixing money from different sources
Coalition – a temporary alliance of factions, parties, and so on for some specific purpose; mobilizes individuals and groups to influence outcomes.
Collaboration – several agencies and organizations working together to achieve project goals and objectives, i.e. schools districts, social service agencies, government agencies, churches, and communities
Commerce Business Daily – Publication of Department of Commerce that announces availability of contracts (RFPs) and recipients of contract awards from the federal government.
Communications – budget category for telephone, telegraph, and similar charges.
Concept paper – a document prepared by the applicant that describes the rationale for a project or the basic idea that might turn into a full proposal; used by some sponsors to screen proposal submissions.
Conference grant- money to underwrite cost of meetings, seminars, etc.

Conference/seminars – money to cover the cost of attending conferences and seminars, planning them, and hosting them; funding may be used to pay for all of the conference's expenses, including securing a keynote speaker, travel, printing, advertising, and facility expenses, such as meals.
Consortium grant- funds funneled to one organization that in turn shares the money with other organizations working jointly on a project.
Consortium- several agencies or organizations joined together for the purpose of submitting a single project application.
Constituency- the group on whose behalf an agency advocates the initiation or continuation of programs or projects intended to improve the condition or reduce the level of need within the constituency.
Construction grant - funds to be used for building, expanding, or modernizing facilities.
Consulting services – these funds are used to secure the expertise of a consultant or consulting firm to strengthen some aspect of organizational programming.
Continuation application - request for funds to continue a funded project that was approved for more than one year contingent upon the availability of funds and satisfactory project operation, requires an annual proposal.
Continuing education grant -funds used to further or to update the training of an individual in a field of importance to the funder.
Continuing support/continuation grant – if you've already received a grant award from a funder, you can return to apply for continuing support.
Contract-legal agreement between the grantee and a grantor of funds specifying the work to be performed, products to be delivered, time schedules, and financial arrangements.
Contractor – organization under a contract to the funder to perform specific work.
Corporate foundation grant- money awarded by a commercial enterprise.
Cost overrun - an increase of the total actual cost over the original estimated cost on a cost-reimbursement contract.
Cost proposal – separate proposal covering the budget, financial, and business aspects of the proposal; also called business proposal.
Cost reimbursement (CR) - contract providing for reimbursement for actual incurred allowable expenditures.
Cost sharing- grant recipient pays a part of the total costs of the project.
Cost-plus contract – contract that provides for reimbursing the contractor for allowable costs that were incurred, plus a fixed a free or amount. Normally used with profit-making organizations; also known as cost-plus fixed-fee contract.
Cover letter – a short letter that accompanies the proposal and briefly describes its significance.
Criteria- the points on which the proposal will be evaluated.

Deadline – date by which the proposal must be received by the funding source or by which it must be postmarked.
Deliverable- to produce or achieve what is desired or expected; make good. Another term for project objectives and outcomes.
Deliverables- the reports, products, research findings, and /or materials that have been promised to or are required by the funding agency by certain dates.
Demographic data- factual information, especially information organized for analysis or used to reason or make decisions.
Demonstration Grant – a grant made to establish a promising and innovative project which, if successful, will serve as a model for replication by others.
Demonstration grant/project- grant or specially funded project to support the demonstration and testing or piloting of a particular approach to education, service delivery, research, training, technical assisting, or other activities.
Denial – the refusal or rejection of a grant request; a refusal letter is usually sent to the application agency/organization; this letter will typically explain why the grant proposal was not awarded funding.
Development team - a group of individuals with specific roles and functions, working toward a specific end-a powerful winning proposal and integrated, implemented project.
Direct assistance - grant providing goods and services (personnel, supplies equipment), not money; in lieu of cash.
Direct costs- total costs directly attributable to the project, including salaries, fringe benefits, travel, equipment, supplies, services, etc; indirect costs are calculated as a percent of the direct costs.
Direct Labor (DL) - total amount to be spent on staff salaries.
Discrepancy model- a method used to compare two or more examples; through this comparison differences reveal characteristic of strong versus weak examples.
Discretionary fund/grant - competitive grant programs in which the applicant designs the project and the funding agency selects projects and determines grant amounts; also called competitive grants or project grants.
Discretionary Funds – grant monies which are allocated according to the funding source's judgment, usually with predetermined priorities.
Dissemination- makes research findings, project outcomes, and products known.
Donation- assistance (financial or in-kind) given to an agency or organization by the private sector without any contractual arrangement.
DUNS (Dun and Bradstreet) Number- a number assigned to an organization that identifies it as a nonprofit agency and establishes its fiscal solvency and credit rating.
Eligible applicants - categories of applicants invited to submit applications, such as institutes of higher, local educational agencies, individuals, private schools, community-based agencies, and public agencies.
Employee benefits - fringe benefits.

Employee matching gifts –many employers match the monetary donations their employees make to nonprofit organizations, often a ratio of 1:1 or 2:1.
Enabling legislation- a law authorizing a grant-making program.
Endowments – a source of long-term, permanent investment income to insure the continuing presence and financial stability of your nonprofit organization.
Entitlement funds - funds allocated primarily on the basis of a formula that seeks to distribute the available funds among recipients in some equitable fashion; funding is not competitive- i.e., all applicants who meet the criteria will be funded.
Evaluation- 1. To ascertain or fix the value or worth of your program, service, reforms, or project; 2. To examine and judge carefully, appraise; 3. A plan for assessing program accomplishments.
Executive summary - a presentation of the substance of a body of material in a condensed form or by reducing it to its main points; an abstract; a very brief usually one-page overview of the proposal.
Exemplar - 1. One that is worthy of imitation; a model. 2. One that is typical or representative, an example; 3. An ideal that serves as a pattern.
E-Z Empowerment Zone –zoning specified by a governmental agency for funding.
FAPRS-(Federal Assistance Program Retrieval System) -computerized system of information on federal funding.
Federal assistance- financial payments by the United States to third parties which entail conditions to be satisfied by the recipient and are in the form of a grant or cooperative agreement.
Federal projects or federal and state projects- general term referring to all categorical funding coming from federal and state funding programs or from federal programs distributed by the state.
Federal Register- daily publication of the U.S. government that announces opportunities to apply for grants and includes regulations.
Fellowship- a grant awarded to an individual to further his/her level of professional competence; money to support a graduate and post-graduate student in specific fields. These funds are only awarded to the institution, never to the individual.
FFP- Federal Financial Participation.
Fiscal Agent – an agency/organization that is responsible for ensuring grant funds are utilized and recorded accurately within specified requirements and guidelines of the funding source.
Fiscal year (FY) - the official accounting period, October 1 through September 30 for the federal government.
Fixed – price contract: agreement to pay a fixed total amount in installments or upon delivery of a product or completion of a scope of work regardless of actual costs of the contractor.

Flow-through money: funds that are funneled through a middleman-(federal funds are funneled through State Departments of Education; also called passed-through funds.

Focus area(s) - a center of interest or activity (e.g., safety, program expansion, curriculum reform, training, staff development.

Formative evaluation - conducted during the operation of a program to assess the outcomes of activities, generally for the purpose of providing immediate feedback and if necessary to effect program change.

Formula grant - funds made available to specified recipients based on a formula prescribed in legislation, regulations, or policies of the agency; states are the chief recipients.

Foundation grant - money awarded by one of 25,000 grant-giving foundations.

Fringe benefits - amount paid by the employer for various employee benefits such as retirement, social security, health insurance, unemployment insurance, disability insurance ,etc., usually included in a budget as a percentage of total salaries; also referred to as employee benefits.

Full-time equivalent (FTE) - combining of part-time positions to show the equivalent number of full-time positions.

Funding Cycle – a chronological framework for proposal submission, review, decision making, applicant notification, and project implementation.

Funding Source – an agency, group, organization, or foundation that has possible funding to grant or contract out to another entity.

GANTT chart – timetable in chart form, showing the various activities included in a proposal, with indication of the length of time elapsing from the start to the end of each activity.

General/operating expenses – money for general budget line-item expenses; these funds may be used for salaries, fringe benefits, travel, consultants, utilities, equipment, and other expenses necessary to operate a nonprofit program.

General Revenue Sharing (GRS) - federal funds given to state and local governments with few restraints on how the money is spent.

Gifts –in-kind: donation for services or goods, no cash

Go/no go – administrative approval or disapproval of the proposal concept and decision to develop proposal by the agency seeking the grant.

Goal – a long range benefit that an individual or group is seeking.

Goals - the purposes toward which an endeavor is directed.

Government grant – usually refers to a grant from the federal government, although state and local governments also make grants.

Grant – a sum of money awarded by any government or private sector financial assistance given to a recipient, individuals, or organization for a particular purpose and time period as detailed in a specific application or proposal; used broadly, may refer to a contract, agreement, or other such document; an award of funds to an agency/or to undertake tax-exempt activities.

Grant Development Team – a group of representatives from various agencies, groups, or populations within a community that can work together in designing and writing a grant proposal.
Grant program – specifically, a project that is funded by a grant broadly used to include projects funded by a contract or agreement.
Grantee – individual, organization, or entity receiving a grant and accountable for that grant.
Grantor – agency (government, foundation, corporation, nonprofit organization, individual) awarding a grant to a recipient; funder.
Grants-management officer – official of a government funding agency or foundation who is designated as the responsible person for the business and financial aspects of a particular grant; this person is usually expected to work in collaboration with the grantor's counterpart of the grantee's business and financial manager.
Grants person – individual responsible for planning, preparing, and marketing proposals.
Grant-supported activities/project – activities specified in a grant application, contract, letter of approval, or other document that are approved by a funding agency as the basis for awarding a grant
Guidelines – set of general principles specified as the basis for judging a proposal; funder's guidelines specify which requirements the proposal must meet with respect to both its content and its form; a statement of goals, priorities, criteria, and procedures for the project that is necessary for funding.
Hard match – requirement that matching funds be a cash contribution or funds not in-kind.
Horizontal/vertical slice – an extended group of people with similar interests or concerns who interact and remain in informal contact for mutual assistance or support.
Impact Evaluation – the measurement of the long-term effectiveness of an activity
Impoundment – situation when the Executive Branch does not spend funds authorized by Congress.
Indirect cost rate – percent of direct costs that has been approved by the government for overhead; a specific formula is used to calculate indirect cost rates.
In-kind contribution – dollar value of noncash contribution to a program by the grantee or a party other than the grantee or grantor; such a contribution usually consists of contributed time of personnel, equipment, supplies, and rent that directly benefit the grant-supported activity.
Instrumentation – tests, questionnaires, etc., to be used to evaluate the project.
Intervention – to come or occur between two periods or points of time.
Joint powers agreement – agreement between two or more agencies that enable one to make use of the resources of the other(s); frequently does not involve the transfer of funds.

Labor intensive – requiring a large expenditure for personnel.
Labor Surplus Set-Aside – solicitations limited to applicants in areas with high unemployment or underemployment according to criteria set by the Secretary of Labor.
Landscape – portrayed as one would a picture depicting an expanse of scenery (11 x 81/2 as opposed to 81/2 x 11).
Lead Agency – the agency or organization that directly receives an award for funds, also known as prime contractor.
Letter of commitment – letter from administrator or governing board that confirms they are committed to the proposed idea and the ideas within it and are willing to commit whatever resources the proposal specifies.
Letter of intent to apply – a brief letter or form you submit to the funding agency; it establishes that you will submit a proposal, and gets you in their information loop for subsequent mailings, workshops, or opportunities.
Letter of support – letter from appropriate stakeholders without whose support the proposed project could not could not be implemented. These letters help to assure the funder that the program is valid and important to the applicants.
Letter proposal – a brief (often preliminary) proposal submitted in letter from, similar to a concept paper.
Level of effort – estimated amount of personnel time required to carry out a project or activity usually expressed in person-years, person-days, person-months, person-weeks, or person-hours.
Leverage – matching funds for a project; amount of money a funder will match for a specific project; this could be a contribution for staffing or in-kind services.
Local government – units of government below the state level such as towns, townships counties, cities, school districts, and federally reorganized Indian Tribal governments.
Maintenance of effort – requirement that the grantee maintain a specific level of activity and financial expenditures in a geographic or program area to ensure that grant funds will not be used to replace (supplant) funds already being spent by the grantee.
Management plan – description usually required in a proposal for how the grantee will relate to the funder and how the project will fit into the district decision-making and government systems.
Manpower loading – proposed schedule of staff/personnel used during the course of the project
Matching funds – grantee's required cash or in-kind contribution to a project, usually a percent of the total budget; grant funds that are awarded with the requirement that you must find other grant funding that matches or exceeds the initial grant's matching-fund stipulation; A grant with specifications that the amount awarded must be matched on a one-for-one basis or some other prescribed formula

Memorandum of Agreement (MOA) – a statement written showing two or more agencies working together with an agreement for the scope of services to be rendered by each agency on the same project.

Memorandum of Understanding (MOU) – An agreement between two agencies; there is an understanding of responsibility between both agencies.

Methods – a description of the programs and services that will achieve the desired results.

Milestones- important events, as in the history of an organization, project, or service, or in the advancement of knowledge in a field, turning points.

Mission- a special assignment or calling by an organization, group, or individual to pursue an activity or perform a service or vocation that addresses a specific need or focus.

Multi-funded- a project supported by two or more funders, usually each a percent of the total budget.

Needs assessment – a questionnaire that seeks information as to the need of a service or product; a compelling description of the need to be addressed by the applicant organization.

Needs statement- a section in the proposal describing and documenting the needs addressed by the proposal.

Negotiations- discussion between the applicant and the funder regarding program and budget changes desired by the funder; negotiations take place before a contract is issued and are becoming more common in relation to discretionary grants.

Network- individuals or organizations formed in a loose-knit group.

New projects- first year of a project

Noncompetitive follow-on - extension of an already existing previously completed contract.

Notice of Funds Availability (NOFA) – a notice of funds availability announced by a funding source, i.e. federal government

Notice of grant award – formal written notice from the funding source notifying of the grant award specifying grant amount, time period, and special requirements.

Objectives – the measurable statements (outcome, deliverables) that demonstrate the growth and reforms being targeted by applicant; usually describe who will do what by when and under what conditions, and how this is measured.

Offeror - organization that is submitting a proposal in response to or bidding on an RFP.

Organization background – a presentation of the organizations qualifications to carry out the proposed project.

Organizational capacity – the ability of your agency to perform or produce; capability. The maximum or optimum amount that can be produced, serviced; innate potential for growth, development, or accomplishment.
Other direct costs – direct costs other than salaries and fringe benefits.
Outcomes – a natural result; a consequence of your grant and the integration and implementation of its methods, activities, and reforms.
Outcome evaluation-The measurement of the short-term effectiveness of an activity
Padding – adding extra amounts to the budget.
Partnership – a relationship between individuals or groups that is characterized by mutual cooperation and responsibility, as for the achievement of a specified goal.
Passed-through funds – funds that are funded through an intermediate agency; also called flow-through funds.
Per diem – daily rate for expenses (other than transportation) incurred while traveling.
Performance contract – specifies levels of performance before the work is considered satisfactory or before the applicant is to be paid by the funder.
Person-years – a concept by which a funding agency attempts to establish cost parameters by defining the scope of a project as the costs of the number of professionals required to do the job, including support costs of clerical and other assistance.
PERT – stands for Program Evaluation Review Technique, which is a schedule of events and activities included in a project indicating the period of time elapsing between events and the relationship of events to each other.
Pilot Project – a brand new project; first time of operation/implementation
Planned variation –p in which funded recipients select from several models which are then evaluated and compared (example: follow through)
Planning grant – grant intended to support activities necessary to design and plan a particular program or project, to design and plan programs in a particular geographic area and/or a particular field of service, or to engage in interagency planning and coordination; planning grants often include research, study, coordination, community participation, community organization, and planning education activities as a component.
Positioning – a point of view or attitude on a certain question or issue that aligns you with the funder's mission, values, vision, and goals.
Preliminary proposal – a brief proposal emphasizing the need and program concept; sometimes requested by funders to screen applicants and save them the task of developing a full proposal if it has little likelihood of funding.
Pre-proposal phase – activities undertaken prior to writing the proposal such as obtaining administrative approval, identifying cooperators, forming an advisory committee, planning, etc.
Prime contractor – agency, organization, or person that directly receives an award of funds with which to accomplish a prescribed scope of work, some of which may be subcontracted.

Principal investigator – usually the researcher responsible for a research project; may be the project director.

Prior approval – approval (usually written) required before a change in the project plan or budget is implemented.

Priorities – the important issues to which an agency or organization is committed to funding or obtaining funding.

Problem statement – the act of stating or declaring one's needs, concerns, liabilities.

Process Evaluation – the measurement of the efficiency or effort put forth in an activity.

Process objective – a description of the specific ways used by the project staff to monitor the project's activities and management scheme.

Product objective – used by funding agencies in two ways: (1) to refer to the behavior expected of project participants, or (2) to refer to a concrete item to be produced by the project, such as a manual or a film.

Program announcement – press release, booklet, catalog, form letter, or notice in the Federal Register telling of an opportunity to apply for a grant or contract.

Program officer – one that supervises, controls, or manages the funds for a philanthropic organization and reports to its governing board; the program officer acts as a community liaison instructing applicants on the guidelines, mission, vision, and values of the funder.

Program/project costs – direct and indirect cost incurred in carrying out a grant-supported program or project; in the case of some grantors, only the cost estimated in the approved budget may be incurred by the grantee as allowable expense related to the grant.

Project director/ program director – individual designated by the grantee to be responsible for the administration of a project; the project director is responsible to the grantee for proper management of the project; the grantee is responsible to the grantor (funder) for submission of all required documents, for maintaining communications between the agencies, and for carrying out all program components as agreed.

Project grant – a general term for a grant supporting a specific project.

Project officer/program officer – The official in a government funding agency or a foundation, who is responsible for a grant program, i.e. supervises technical and program aspects of grants; may also be responsible for administrative and fiscal aspects.

Project period – local time over which a grant is to be expended.

Project Scope – the amount effort to be expended in conducting the activities of a project; scope may be expressed in terms of total dollar cost, the size of the target group, project procedures, or manpower utilization including the number of person years to be required.

Proposal – formal written document that provides detailed information to a funder on the conduct and cost of a proposed project.

Provider – an individual or organization who contractually agrees to provide services.

Qualitative – 1. expressed or expressible as a quantity; 2. of, relating to, or susceptible of measurement; 3. of or relating to number or quantity.

Quality Assurance – ensure that the agency is in compliance with rules and regulations set forth by the funder; a set of standards for the organization.

Rationale – section of a proposal justifying the proposed solution.

Regulations – rules developed by federal agencies to implement laws passed by state legislatures.

Reimbursement formula – formula for providing funds based on population, services rendered proportion of budget to be provided by grantee, etc.; relates to the methods and activities employed during proposal implementation.

Renewal grant – a project that has been previously funded; rewrite and resubmit grant to the same funder for another round of funding, a continuation program.

Research grant – grant to support research in the form of studies, surveys, evaluations, investigations, experimentation; money to support medical and educational research; monies are usually awarded to the institutions that employ the individuals who will be conducting the research.

Revenue sharing – federal program providing assistance to states and localities for broad general purposes and with limited federal control.

Reviewer's comments – ratings and explanation of ratings of the panelists who reviewed a proposal.

RFP – stands for "Request for Proposal", The application for a grant or the notice of the grant availability which is a formal announcement from a funding agency inviting the submission of a proposal and specifying the requirements that the proposal must meet with respect to the objectives, scope of work, work plan, administration, timing, and reporting.

Rubric – a score form provided by the funding agency to help readers form an opinion or evaluation of the proposed project and how it positions itself against the agency's guidelines.

Scholarship funds – scholarships are awards to individuals.

Seed money – grants to encourage the grantee to start a new program which the funder expects will eventually become self-sustaining or will be supported by the grantee; a grant awarded to start a new project by an agency organization.

SGA - Solicitation for Grant Application. Each application contains sections called summary and supplemental background information.

Sign-Off – the securing of approval or acknowledgement that a designated state or regional agency has been informed about the submission of a grant proposal

Site visit – visit by one or more persons responsible to the funding agency to the site of the submitter of a proposal in order to obtain additional evaluative information on the basis of firsthand observation and discussion.

Soft match – Matching funds may be in-kind contributions.

Sole Source – Agency or organization considered by the funder to be the only available resource to fulfill the requirements of a proposed contract.
Solicited proposal – A proposal that has in some way been invited by a sponsoring agency; a proposal in response to an RFP or a program announcement inviting applications; a formal invitation of a funder.
Special projects or specially funded projects – used to distinguish those parts of the total educational program supported by special purpose funds from those supported by the general fund.
Sponsor – usually means funder.
Staff loading analysis – estimate of staff time needed for each task.
Stakeholders – 1. the party for which professional services are rendered; 2. a customer, client, or beneficiary; 3. a person using the services of your organization.
Statement of purpose – a declaration of result or an effect that is intended or desired; an intention.
Stipend – payment to an individual, usually to support living costs while participating in a training or fellowship program.
Subcontract – an arrangement whereby the prime sponsor or the direct recipient of a sponsor's funds agrees to use the services of another agency or organization (usually contractually) in carrying out some portion of the proposed activities.
Summative evaluation – description or measurement of final program results.
Supplemental monies – monies are appropriated by Congress for programs that were not included in the regular appropriation bill.
Survey – an instrument used to gather statistical data.
Sustainability – how the program or project will continue to receive funding after the initial funding has ended; other funding resources
Systematic – carried on using step-by-step procedures; purposefully regular; methodical.
Systemic – relating to, or affecting the entire organization, its stakeholders, clients, community, and support network.
Target group – a specified group or category of persons for whom the project has been developed and whose needs are intended to be affected by the proposed activities.
Technical assistance (TA) projects – projects that support the provision of services to specified agencies or projects; services are designed to help practitioners implement a program.
Technical proposal – used by some government agencies to refer to the narrative proposal covering all aspects of the proposal except the budget and business information, which are included in a separate business proposal; this procedure is commonly used in responses to RFPs leading to a contract.

Third Party – agency, organization, or individual other than the funder or grantee who is involved in a supported project; often a subcontractor.
Time and material contract – fixed daily or hourly rate for each staff member with direct project expenses charged at cost; periodic payments.
Timeline – a management tool that graphically shows the task to be accomplished, by whom, and over what estimated period of time.
Training grant – supports training of staff, students, prospective employees, project participants, or a designated population.
Unobligated balance – amount remaining of a grant at the end of the grant period against which there will be no expenses. Such balances, at the discretion of the grantor, may have to be returned, or they may be used as a deduction from the next grant (a continuation) if there is one, or carried over to the next continuation period as addition to the next grant.
Unsolicited proposal – initiated by the applicant; not in response to an announcement soliciting proposals or an RFP.
Value – worth in usefulness or importance of your program or project to the funding agency; utility or merit.
Values – beliefs and priorities of the applicant expressed and reflected in the proposal.
Vision – the central idea to which the applicant is committed through the grant proposal.
Wired – term indicating that the selection of an organization to receive a grant has been decided prior to the submission of competitive proposals.

Glossary source: Robert Lefferts /*Getting a Grant in the 1980's* (1982)

Jim Burke & Carole Ann Prater, *I'll Grant You That* (2000) gives credit to John and Ruthmary Cordon-Cradler for creating the glossary in I'll Grant You That". (2000).

Bibliography

Brown & Brown, *Demystifying Grant Seeking*, Jossey-Bass, San Francisco, CA 2001

Browning, B. *Grant writing for Dummies*, New York Hungry Minds, Inc. 2001

Burke, J & Prather, *I'll Grant You That*, Heinemann, Portsmouth, NH, 2000

Carlson, M. *Winning Grants*, Step By Step, Second edition, John Wiley & Son, Inc. 2002

Department of the Treasury Internal Revenue Service Publication 1828, www.irs.gov 2009

Department of the Treasury Internal Revenue Service Publications 4220, applying for 501(c)(3) *tax-exempt status for nonprofit organizations*, www.irs.gov *2009*

Department of the Treasury Internal Revenue Service Publication 1771, *Charitable Contributions*, www.irs.gov 2009

Lefferts, R. *Getting a Grant in the 1980's*, Second edition, Prentice-Hall., Englewood Cliffs, NJ 1982

Price, R.W., *Roadmap to Entrepreneurial Success*, AMACOM-American Management Association, New York, NY 2004

New, C, & Quick, J. *Grantseeker's Toolkit*, John Wiley & Sons, Inc. New York, NY 1998

Website: http://en.Wikipedia.org/Wiki/Foundation (non-profit) Main Article: Foundation (USA) 2010

Website: http://foundationcenter.org/getstarted/faqs/html/foundfun.html *What is a foundation?* 2010

Webster's New Pocket Dictionary, Wiley Publishing, Inc. Cleveland, Ohio 2000